QUILTS ON THE DOUBLE

Dozens of Easy Strip-Pieced Designs

JUDY HOOWORTH &
MARGARET ROLFE

Martingale®
& COMPANY

Quilts on the Double: Dozens of Easy
Strip-Pieced Designs
© 2008 by Judy Hooworth and Margaret Rolfe

That Patchwork Place® is an imprint of
Martingale & Company®.

Martingale & Company
20205 144th Ave. NE
Woodinville, WA 98072-8478 USA
www.martingale-pub.com

Credits

President & CEO ~ Tom Wierzbicki
Publisher ~ Jane Hamada
Editorial Director ~ Mary V. Green
Managing Editor ~ Tina Cook
Technical Editor ~ Ellen Pahl
Copy Editor ~ Durby Peterson
Design Director ~ Stan Green
Assistant Design Director ~ Regina Girard
Illustrator ~ Adrienne Smitke
Cover & Text Designer ~ Stan Green
Photographer ~ Brent Kane & David Paterson

Printed in China
13 12 11 10 09 08   8 7 6 5 4 3 2 1

Library of Congress Cataloging-in-Publication Data
Library of Congress Control Number: 2007030503
ISBN: 978-1-56477-778-2

Acknowledgments

Judy is immensely grateful to Margaret for her clear vision and
expertise in the realization of this book; it would never have happened
without her!

Judy's concept has had a long gestation and she thanks her
students, who attended classes and gave input over the years. Judy is
grateful to Diana Marshall and the students from the Oatley Cottage
Annual Patchwork Seminar for their willing participation in the
development of her ideas and for the wonderful quilts they created.
Particular thanks to Roslyn Dickens, Wendy Knight, Heidi Nixon,
Helene Saunders, Jeanie Atkinson, Maureen Bench, Georgina Cleaver,
Heather Joyce, Barbara McNamara, and Edwina Rich. Thanks also
to Kerrie Hay and the team from Bernina Australia for their ongoing
support.

Margaret thanks Judy for the invitation to help develop her original
idea into a book, and for offering another enjoyable opportunity to
work together. She thanks her husband, Barry, for his never-failing
support for yet another book. She is also grateful for the quilting of
Shawly Sensational in finishing two of her quilts.

Both Margaret and Judy wish to thank Martingale & Company for
publishing this book, and David Paterson for his photography of the
quilts. Anne Eccleston generously helped with the reading of the book
proofs.

They also gratefully acknowledge the support of Tanya White from
3M for supplying Thinsulate batting, which suited their quilts perfectly.

MISSION STATEMENT
Dedicated to providing quality products and service to inspire creativity.

CONTENTS

Page 25

Page 62

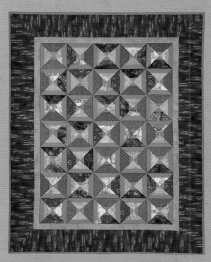

Page 78

INTRODUCTION

Come, take a journey with us and explore the possibilities of making two quilts from one set of fabrics using simple cutting and sewing! You'll have "quilts on the double" because you will make two quilts from some basic quick piecing.

We would like to stress at the beginning that making the quilts in this book is like taking a journey, but it is a journey in which you discover your own destination. After choosing your fabrics, you will begin with straightforward strip piecing. You will proceed to make some diagonal cuts that give you two sets of triangles. Everyone will take these same beginning steps. But after this, the fun begins as you arrange these triangles to make two quilts. There are many, many possibilities for each quilt, so your journey will be unique as you explore the alternatives to find the destination that works best for your own set of fabrics.

And then there is more! The leftover triangles may be used to make a small bonus quilt. Nothing, but nothing, is wasted.

While on the journey of making these quilts, you will learn lots about creating quilts. You will come to new understanding through doing, which is the best way to learn. You will see how to create different patterns by arranging the triangles in different ways. These triangles can create patterns by remaining as they are, by becoming larger triangles, or by being combined to make squares or diamonds. In short, they can be arranged to make many different block designs. Yet simplicity is the order of the day, because most blocks will have only 8 pieces in them, with a few block possibilities containing a maximum of 12 pieces. The designs work especially well with striped fabrics, because you can make all kinds of Log Cabin patterns with stripes.

Groups of fat quarters or fat eighths form the basis of the quilts. This book may help you use up some of your stash!

These quilts on the double are ideal projects to do with a friend. Get together for making the Doubles triangles; then enjoy creating two quite different quilts from this simple beginning. We did this with our "Primary Colors" quilts (see page 80), and had a lot of fun together. With the Internet, you can even do this long distance, by emailing images back and forth.

In this book we first describe the concept—how some strip piecing and cutting can result in three groups of triangles. We show you the amazing possibilities that can result when the triangles are arranged into patterns. Then we include the nitty-gritty of choosing the fabrics, measuring for cutting, and doing the simple but accurate sewing required. A group of our quilts follows, with complete instructions, showing how some of the possibilities work in the fabrics we have chosen. We have provided galleries of quilts to inspire you and give even more ideas. Last, we've included a section with the how-to basics of patchwork and quilt assembly, a reference for those times when you need it.

We urge you first to look at the quilts to see and enjoy the amazing variety that can be created from one simple idea! Then read about the concept and look at the diagrams that show you even more possibilities. After this, review the details in the how-to section and quilt instructions. We want you to enjoy your journey as you play with the possibilities in your fabrics and make quilts that are your very own.

THE DOUBLES CONCEPT

The concept is based on choosing two groups of contrasting fabrics and adding one accent fabric.

Don't worry about the specifics of all this at the moment, because we'll come to that later. For now, just take in the general ideas.

- Choose two groups of contrasting fabrics.

- Choose an accent fabric.

- Cut the two groups of contrasting fabrics into wide strips.

- Cut the accent fabric into narrow strips.

- Sew a strip of the accent fabric to each strip from the two contrasting groups.

- Cut the strip sets into triangles.

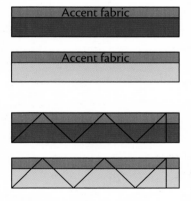

We call the triangles with little caps of accent fabric the *Tops*. We call the triangles with the strip of accent fabric at the bottom of the triangle the *Tails*. We call the leftover triangles at the side the *Sides*. These are a bonus! Thus the simple

cutting and sewing will give you three groups of triangles: a group of Tops, a group of Tails, and a group of Sides.

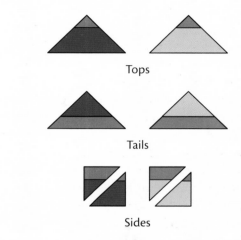

Tops

Tails

Sides

ARRANGING THE TRIANGLES

Now the fun really begins! Take your sets of triangles to a design wall and begin to play! In the sections that follow are just some of the possible arrangements.

Arranging Tops

There are four different ways that the triangles can be arranged to make Tops blocks. These four possibilities can make all kinds of quilt designs. Placing the blocks on point gives even further possibilities. See pages 6 and 7 for sample quilt designs.

Tops blocks

STRAIGHT-SET QUILT DESIGNS USING THE TOPS BLOCKS

ON-POINT QUILT DESIGNS USING THE TOPS BLOCKS

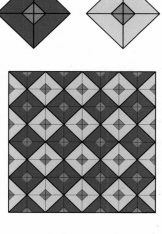

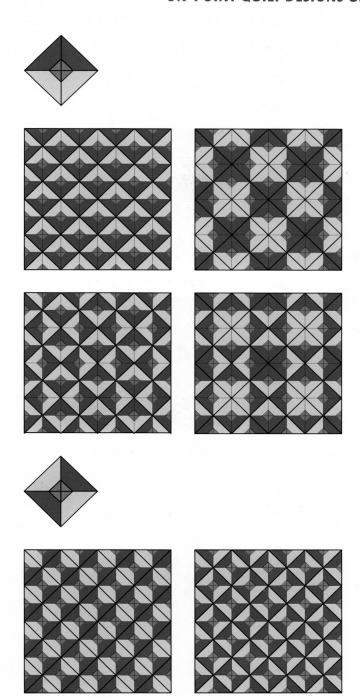

Light accent

Medium accent

Dark accent

Note that the illustrations show a medium value to indicate the accent color, but this may also be a light or dark value. There are just too many possibilities to include them all!

Arranging Tails

There are also four different possibilities for arranging the triangles to make Tails blocks.

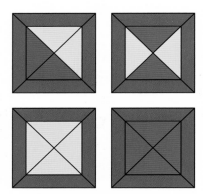

Many more possibilities can be created by adding triangles made of an additional, or background, fabric to Tails triangles or to Tails triangles sewn together.

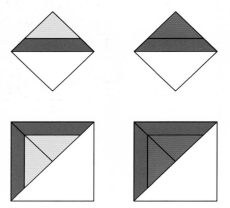

The Tails blocks can work well with the addition of alternate blocks of fabric between the blocks. The addition of sashing strips and cornerstones gives more possibilities. Putting any of the arrangements on point also gives a new look. Note that when the blocks are arranged on point, they will usually require setting triangles at the sides and corners of the quilt.

TAILS QUILT DESIGNS

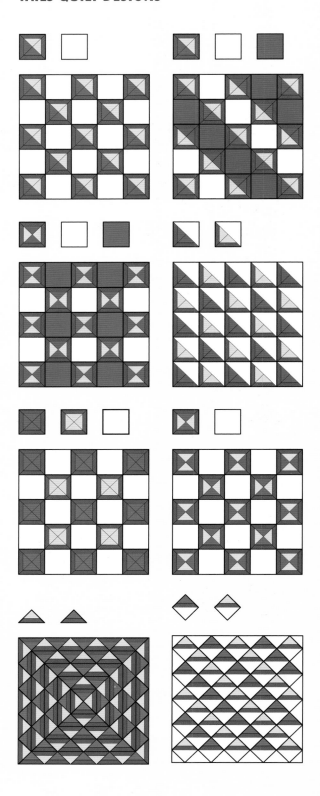

Combinations

Combination quilts are made using both Tops and Tails triangles. They can be made of blocks that contain both Tops and Tails triangles, or they can combine Tops blocks and Tails blocks.

In these quilts also, there are lots more possible arrangements. All the quilt designs shown here could also be put on point, but there's not enough space to show you all the options. Note that when using a Combination design, it is possible to make one large quilt instead of two different quilts.

Combination blocks

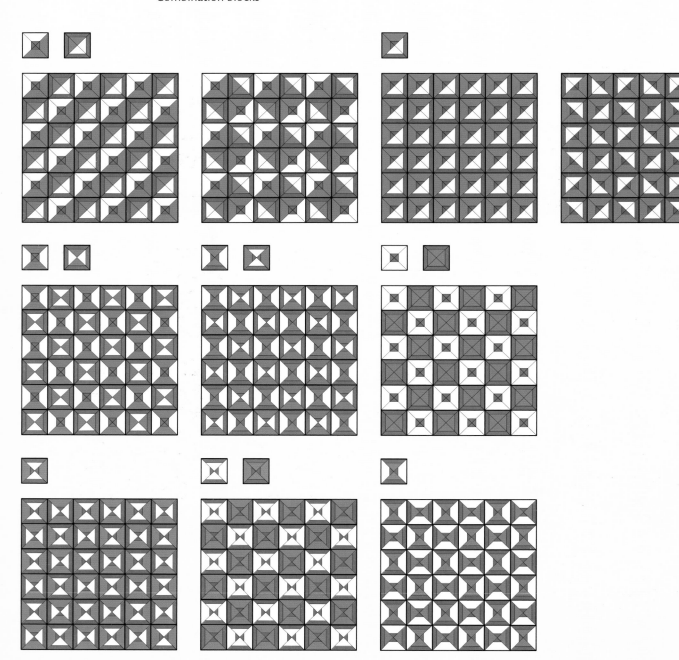

Arranging Sides

The Sides triangles are an extra bonus that can make several different blocks. Note that right- and left-handed quilters will have Sides triangles that are mirror images of each other. It depends on which end of the strip set you begin your cutting. (See "Cutting the Doubles Triangles" on page 18 for additional information.) Either way, you will have Sides-Tops triangles and Sides-Tails triangles.

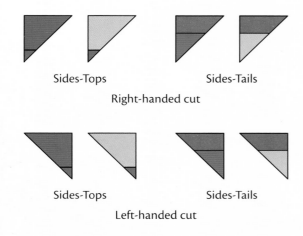

Sides-Tops · Sides-Tails

Right-handed cut

Sides-Tops · Sides-Tails

Left-handed cut

Similar to the Tails triangles, Sides triangles work well when they are combined with triangles of a background fabric.

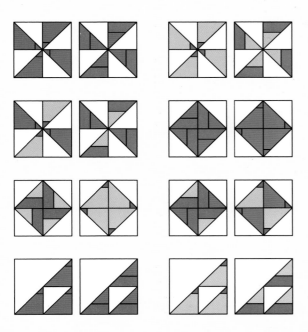

Here are just a few of the possibilities for these blocks. The arrangements for the blocks will be the same whether the blocks are cut by right-handed or left-handed quilters, although they will be a mirror image of each other. Here we show triangles as they appear when cut right-handed.

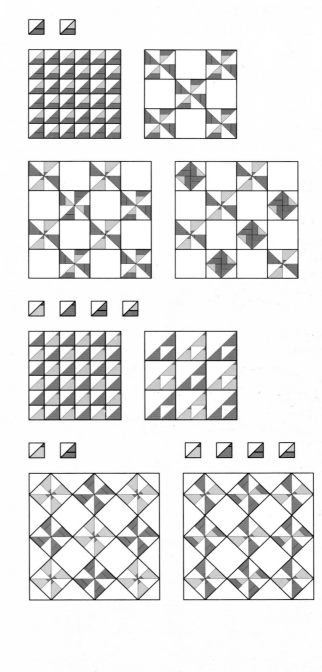

CHOOSING FABRICS

Here we come to how you choose the fabrics for the Doubles triangles. First we'll look at the quantities involved and then we'll look at the factors that will help you make your choices.

The Doubles triangles are based on a set of fabrics made up of three parts:

1. A group of six fat quarters, or their equivalent. A fat quarter measures a minimum of 18" x 20". You can also use the equivalent of six fat quarters, such as 12 fat eighths, where a fat eighth measures a minimum of 9" x 20". Another equivalent to a fat quarter is a quarter-yard piece, which measures a minimum of 9" x 40".

2. A second group of six fat quarters that contrast with the first group. As with the first group, fat eighths or quarter yards can be used as equivalents.

3. An accent fabric that will complement the two groups of fabrics. You will need 1⅞ yards of accent fabric to make the Doubles triangles. Generally you may want to reintroduce the accent fabric into the borders and bindings, so if you are designing your own quilts, we suggest that you purchase more than this quantity.

CREATING THE CONTRAST

When choosing the two groups of fat quarters for these quilts, it is important to choose two groups of fabrics that will contrast well with each other. There are three basic characteristics of fabric: color, value, and print style. Use these to help you create the contrast between your groups of fabrics.

Color. Color is usually the most obvious characteristic of a fabric. Thus you have red fabrics, blue fabrics, yellow fabrics, and so on. Remember, though, that each color can contain nuances of other colors. For example, a red can be a light or dark red, or it can be a blue-tinged or an orange-tinged red.

A range of red fabrics

FABRIC QUANTITIES

Fat quarters, fat eighths, and quarter yards are named after the way the fabric is cut from a yard. Fabrics are usually about 42" wide, of which 40" is usable.

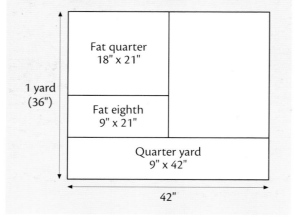

COLOR CONTRAST: *You can make the contrast through color, such as a group of yellow fabrics contrasted with a group of blue fabrics, a group of red fabrics contrasted with a group of black fabrics, or a group of black-and-white fabrics contrasted with a group of orange fabrics.*

Value. *Value* simply means how light or dark a fabric looks. Pure white is obviously the lightest possibility, and pure black is the darkest. Everything else falls somewhere between these two, whether the fabric is black and white, one color, or multiple colors.

Light-to-dark value ranges in black and white, purple, and multiple colors.

Remember that value can be relative. The same fabric may be considered lighter in some cases and darker in others, depending on the fabrics it is placed next to. This applies particularly to fabrics with a medium value, because these fabrics can appear lighter or darker depending on the value of their neighbors.

RELATIVE VALUE: *Look at how the fabric at the top left is light in the top row, medium in the middle row, and dark in the bottom row.*

If you choose to make a contrast through value, one group of fabrics will be lighter in color and the other group will be darker.

VALUE CONTRAST: *In each group, light fabrics are at left and dark fabrics at right.*

Print style. The print style is the pattern of the fabric. There are all kinds of print styles, such as stripes, checks, geometric designs, florals, small-scale patterns, large-scale patterns, sparse patterns, allover patterns, realistic motifs, and so on.

PRINT STYLES: The range is as diverse as the human imagination can create.

There are also fabrics without any pattern: the solids. We have used a lot of these, because they are ideal for accent fabrics. They can also be effectively used as one of the groups of fabric.

SOLIDS: There are so many wonderful colors to choose from!

The print style can also be used to create a contrast, for example, stripes contrasting with a completely different kind of print, such as a tone-on-tone print.

PRINT-STYLE CONTRAST: Mottled solids at left and stripes at right.

Any one of the three characteristics can also enhance contrast between the other two. For example, fabrics that contrast in color, such as a group of yellow fabrics and a group of blue fabrics, will also differ in value because yellow is generally a lighter color than blue. A marked difference between the print styles also enhances a contrast in value or color. For example, if you are choosing two groups of fabrics that differ in value, you can strengthen the contrast by choosing fabrics in one group with a similar kind of pattern, such as stripes or florals, to contrast with solids or tone-on-tone fabrics in the second group.

CHOOSING THE ACCENT FABRIC

Choose a solid (a plain-colored fabric), a tone-on-tone print (a print containing several tones of one color), or a print with a small-scale pattern (small dots, for example). You could also use a hand-dyed fabric or one printed to look hand-dyed. The accent can be any color or value (light, medium, or dark) that suits your two particular groups of fabrics.

MAKING DOUBLES TRIANGLES

The basic steps to making Doubles triangles are quite simple: cut strips, sew them together to make strip sets, and then cut triangles from the strip sets. In this section you will also find information about using striped fabrics to make the Doubles triangles.

CUTTING THE STRIPS

For standard rotary-cutting techniques, refer to page 88.

Cutting Strips from the Accent Fabric

The accent fabric will be full width, anywhere from 40" to 42" wide. Fold the fabric in half lengthwise and cut across the width.

From the accent fabric, cut:
36 strips, 1⅝" wide; cut each strip in half to make a total of 72 strips, 1⅝" x approximately 21". Make counting easy by cutting the strips in groups of 6.

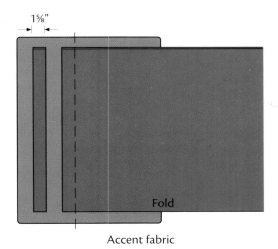

Accent fabric

Cutting Strips from the Contrasting Fabrics

The cutting instructions for the groups of contrasting fabrics are based on fat quarters, or their equivalents in fat eighths and quarter yards.

Cut each fabric across the widest part (when using stripes, there may be exceptions to this; see "Using Stripes" on page 16). Speed up the cutting by layering two fabrics so that you cut 2 strips at one time.

You will cut a total of 36 strips from each group of fabrics, making a grand total of 72 strips.

From each fat quarter, cut:
6 strips, 2¾" wide. You will need 6 fat quarters to cut 36 strips.

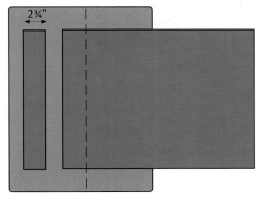

Contrasting fabrics

From each fat eighth, cut:
3 strips, 2¾" wide. You will need 12 fat eighths to cut 36 strips.

From each quarter yard, fold the fabric in half and cut:
3 strips, 2¾" wide. Cut each strip in half. You will need 6 quarter yards to cut 36 strips.

SUMMARY OF CUTTING

From the accent fabric, cut:
36 strips, 1⅝" wide; cut each strip in half to make a total of 72 strips

From the 2 groups of contrasting fabrics, cut:
6 strips, 2¾" wide, from each fat quarter
OR 3 strips, 2¾" wide, from each fat eighth
OR 3 strips, 2¾" wide, from each quarter yard and cut each strip in half. There will be 36 strips from each group of fabrics for a total of 72.

Note: See special instructions in "Using Stripes" (below).

USING STRIPES

Stripes are especially good to use in these quilts because they can give you all kinds of interesting effects in a Log Cabin style. However, because of the different ways that stripes are printed on the fabric, they may need special handling when cutting.

Stripes can be printed on fabric in various ways. Most stripes are printed along the length of the fabric with the stripes running parallel to the selvages. Some stripes go across the width of the fabric, from one selvage edge across to the other.

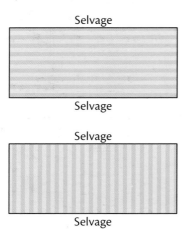

Selvage

Occasionally stripes are printed so that they run diagonally across the fabric. We suggest that you use these diagonally striped fabrics as any other print, which means that the stripes will run diagonally next to the strip of accent fabric. Diagonal stripes can be a very lively addition to a quilt, but be aware that sometimes they may be a little too lively and may have to be abandoned! A group of diagonally striped fabrics could be very effective, however. Just don't cut strips on the bias following the diagonal stripes, because the strips will have too much stretch.

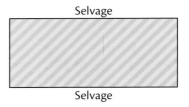

Lengthwise and widthwise stripes can be used in two different ways in the quilts. First, the stripes can be parallel to the strip of accent fabric; in other words, the stripes will go in the same direction as the accent fabric. Second, the stripes can be perpendicular to the strip of accent fabric; in other words, the stripes will be at right angles to the accent fabric.

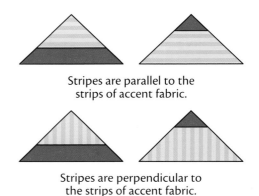

Stripes are parallel to the strips of accent fabric.

Stripes are perpendicular to the strips of accent fabric.

Stripes and Fat Quarters

When using fat quarters, a problem may arise with striped fabrics. This is due to the nature of fat quarters, which are rectangles that measure 18" by approximately 21". A full 20"-long strip is required to get two Tops and two Tails from each strip set; cutting across an 18" width results in only two Tops and one Tails triangle. This problem with striped fabrics arises in two situations:

First situation. This occurs when you have stripes going down the length of the fabric and you want the stripes to be parallel to the strip of accent fabric.

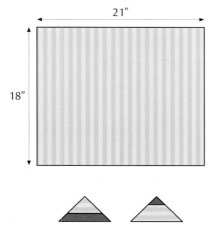

Second situation. This occurs when you have stripes going across the width of the fabric and you want the stripes to be perpendicular to the strip of accent fabric.

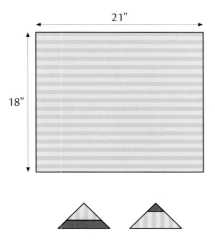

Solution A (works in both situations). Purchase ⅝ yard of the striped fabric. Cut the piece in half and use one half in place of a fat quarter, leaving the remaining half for another project.

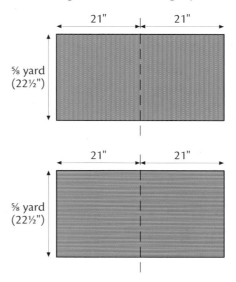

Solution B (works in both situations). Cut two Tops and one Tails triangle as usual. Piece the second Tails triangle from the leftover pieces (otherwise used to create Sides triangles). To do this, cut strips across the shorter side of the fat quarter (you'll be able to cut seven strips rather than six). Sew the accent fabric to six of the strips. Then cut out the triangles, cutting two full Tops triangles and one full Tails triangle from each strip set, but *not* cutting Sides triangles as usual.

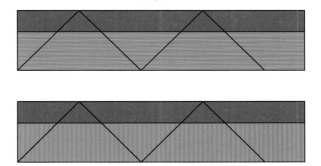

Trim an exact right angle as close as possible to each end of the remaining pieces. Re-press the seam allowance of one of the pieces in the opposite direction and join the pieces, butting the seams together. Press the joining seam open. Trim to make a Tails triangle. The stripes may not match perfectly, but don't worry if they don't. Remember, this is patchwork! Women have always pieced patches in their quilts so that fabric is used economically. Use the seventh strip to create Sides triangles, if desired, although you will need to cut an extra strip of accent fabric.

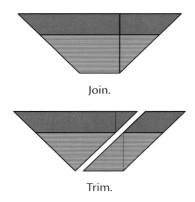

Join.

Trim.

Note: Do not use striped fat eighths if the stripes go down the length of the fabric and you wish them to be parallel to the strip of accent fabric.

MAKING THE STRIP SETS

Using an exact ¼" seam allowance, sew a 1⅝"-wide strip of accent fabric to each of the 2¾"-wide strips to make 72 strip sets. *Using a dry iron,* press the seam allowances of one group of fabrics toward the accent fabric and press the seam allowances of the other group of fabrics away from the accent fabric. When pressing, first press along the seam line with right sides together to flatten the strips. Then open out the sewn strips and gently press from the right side.

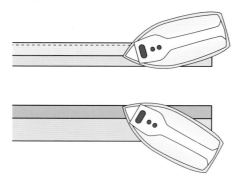

Why Use a Dry Iron?

We recommend using a dry iron for pressing because you do not want to lock the seam allowances to one side at this point, which is what pressing with steam will do. It's important to have the option of changing the pressing direction later on when you sew the triangles together. The triangles will sew together very easily when the seam allowances are pressed in opposite directions. At this stage, however, you do not yet know which block arrangement you will choose.

CUTTING THE DOUBLES TRIANGLES

The Doubles triangles are quarter-square triangles with one long edge on the straight grain and two shorter bias edges. To cut triangles from each of the strip sets, you will need either a 6" or 6½" square ruler or a ruler specially designed for cutting quarter-square triangles.

You can speed up the process by cutting two, or even three, strip sets at once. Lay a strip set horizontally across the cutting mat, with the *right side of the fabrics facing up* and the accent fabric away from you. Lay a second strip on top of the first strip, *again right side up* but with the accent fabric near you so that the seams are not on top of one another. Carefully align the top and bottom edges of the two strip sets as you lay down the second strip. Depending on how much strength your hands have for cutting, you may lay a third strip on top with the accent fabric away from you, again placing the fabric right side up and carefully aligning the edges of the strips.

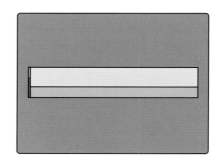

1. Straighten one end by making a right-angle cut. If you are right-handed, trim and begin cutting at the left end of the strips; if you are left-handed, trim and begin cutting at the right end of the strips.

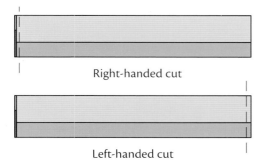

Right-handed cut

Left-handed cut

2. **If you are using a 6" square ruler:** Find the 0" corner of the ruler, the corner between the two 1" marks. With the strip set in front of you, place the ruler on point so that the 0" corner of the ruler aligns with the top edge of the strip set. Move the ruler around until the 5½" mark on each side aligns with the bottom edge of the strip set.

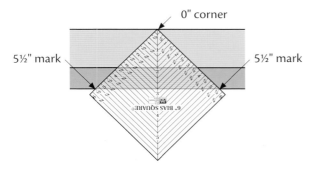

If you are using a quarter-square triangle ruler: With the strip set in front of you, place the ruler so that the tip of the triangle ruler aligns with the top of the strip set; the 6½" mark on the ruler should align with the bottom edge of the strip set.

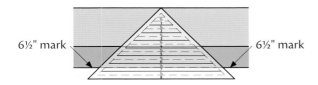

3. **For both rulers:** Keeping the measurements in place, move the ruler along until the lower edge of the ruler meets the lower corner of the strip set (which is on the left end for right-handed people or the right end for left-handed people). Cut along the edges of the ruler to cut the first triangle (1) from the layered strip sets. Turn the ruler around and cut the second triangle (2). Repeat the turning and cutting for the third and fourth triangles. Lastly, trim the other end to make a right angle, cutting vertically to meet the tip of the last triangle.

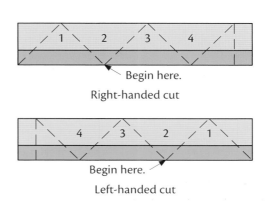

Right-handed cut

Left-handed cut

Your cutting will make two Tops triangles, two Tails triangles, and two Sides triangles from each strip set. Note that the Sides triangles cut by right-handed people are a mirror image of the Sides triangles cut by left-handed people.

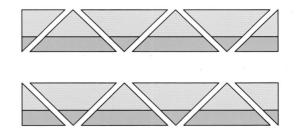

In total, you will cut 72 Tops triangles and 72 Tails triangles from each group of fabrics, making a grand total of 144 Tops and 144 Tails. There will also be 72 Sides-Tops triangles and 72 Sides-Tails triangles.

The finished Tops and Tails block size is 6½" x 6½"; the unfinished size is 7" x 7". All the blocks are pieced by simply sewing four triangles together. Note that you should decide your block design and layout before sewing triangles into pairs.

1. Sew the triangles into pairs, and then sew these pairs together. Be careful to maintain an exact ¼" seam allowance, especially as you sew into the sharp angled corners. As with any quarter-square triangles, remember that the diagonal edges are cut on the bias; handle them carefully.

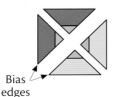

Bias edges

2. Trim away the little excess triangles of seam allowance at the corners.

Trim.

PRESSING TIPS

The triangles will easily sew together with exact junctions at the seams, *provided you press the seam allowances in opposite directions at each junction.* It is worth taking the trouble to re-press the seam allowances to ensure that they always lie in opposite directions at junctions. This will make the sewing both easy and accurate. It is

for this reason we recommend pressing the strip sets with a dry iron, enabling you to change the direction of the seam allowances as needed.

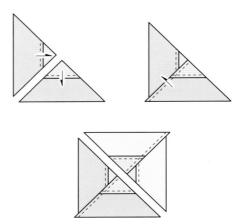

Make a trial block to find out which direction to press the seam allowances, and then press them in exactly the same manner for all the triangles before you begin to sew the blocks together. Organize the triangles so that you sew the pairs of triangles in exactly the same way each time. Chain piecing adds efficiency.

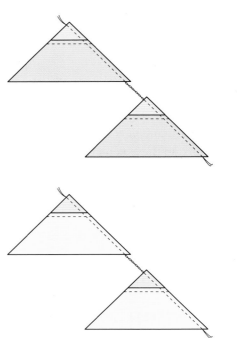

After you have created the Doubles triangles, the excitement really begins as you explore ways that you can use them. We suggest that you look at the quilts throughout the book for inspiration, and see also "Arranging the Triangles" (beginning on page 5) for more ideas. Every group of fabrics will be unique in its composition, combining a variety of colors, values, and print styles. Try out different arrangements on your design wall till you are happy with one that works for your group of fabrics.

Look at the combinations from a distance when deciding on a design. A reducing glass, a camera, or binoculars used backward can help. If you have a digital camera, try taking photos of various arrangements. You don't have to keep or print these photos, but the images may help you choose among the alternatives.

One of the first steps in making the quilts is to choose whether you want to pair the triangles from your two groups within all the blocks. If you wish to pair the fabrics in the blocks, decide which fabrics go best together to create the contrast you envision; then maintain this pairing for all the blocks. See this approach in "Beach Brollies: Tops Quilt" (page 25). The alternative is to mix up the prints within the blocks, and this can be done in two ways. One way is to mix up *all* the prints within the blocks so that each block has four different prints, two from each group, as in "South Pacific: Tops Quilt" (page 51). The other way is to maintain *pairs* from each group of fabrics but mix up these pairs throughout the blocks. Each block has two pairs of prints within it, but the pairs are in different combinations from one block to the next. See this in "Vaudeville: Tops Quilt" (page 67).

Quilts using the Tails and Sides triangles may incorporate background fabrics for even more options when designing quilts. The background fabric can be used for triangles that are sewn to the Tails or Sides triangles or for alternate blocks. Read on for information on cutting sizes to help when planning quilts that use background fabrics.

CUTTING SIZES FOR BACKGROUND FABRICS

For the quilts in this book, we've used alternate blocks and background triangles only with the Tails and Sides blocks.

Tails Blocks

The finished Tails block size is 6½" x 6½"; the unfinished size is 7" x 7" (this includes seam allowances).

Alternate blocks. Cut 7" squares.

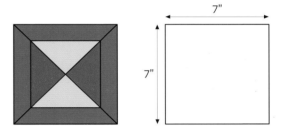

Half-square triangles to match the blocks. Cut 7⅜" squares; then cut the squares in half diagonally.

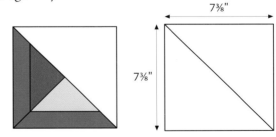

Half-square triangles to match the triangles. Cut 5½" squares; then cut the squares in half diagonally. (Note that the short sides of these triangles will be on the straight grain. The short sides of the Tails triangles will be on the bias; handle them carefully.)

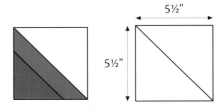

Blocks on point. The diagonal measurement of each block is 9¼", finished size. Half of a block measures 4⅝".

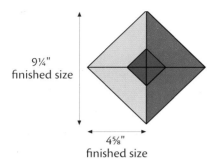

Side and corner setting triangles. Cut 10½" squares; then cut the squares diagonally twice for side triangles. (These triangles will give you the straight grain along the outer edges of the quilt center.) Cut 5½" squares; then cut the squares in half diagonally for corner triangles.

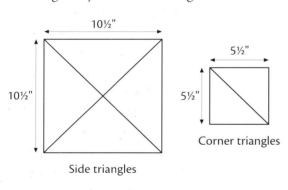

Side triangles

Corner triangles

Sides Blocks

The finished block size is 3" x 3"; the unfinished size is 3½" x 3½" (including seam allowances).

Half-square triangles to match the triangles. Cut 3⅞" squares; then cut the squares in half diagonally.

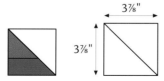

Alternate blocks. Cut 3½" squares.

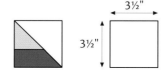

Blocks made up of four Sides triangles have a finished block size of 6" x 6"; the unfinished size is 6½" x 6½" (including seam allowances).

Alternate blocks. Cut 6½" squares.

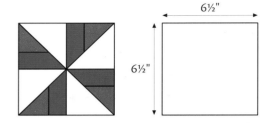

Half-square triangles to match the blocks. Cut 6⅞" squares; then cut the squares in half diagonally.

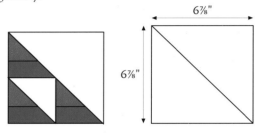

Blocks on point. The diagonal measurement of blocks made of four Sides triangles is 8½", finished size; half of a block measures 4¼".

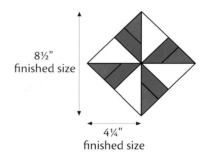

Side and corner setting triangles. Cut 9¾" squares; then cut the squares diagonally twice for side triangles. Cut 5⅛" squares; then cut the squares in half diagonally for corner triangles.

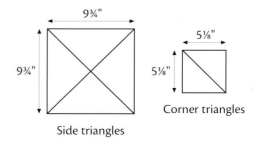

Side triangles

Corner triangles

In this section are quilts that we made when exploring the possibilities of Doubles triangles. We hope they will inspire you!

There are three parts to this section. The first part includes pairs of Tops and Tails quilts. In each pair, one quilt was made from the Tops triangles, and the other was made from the Tails triangles. The second part includes a pair of quilts made using combinations of Tops and Tails triangles. If you use the Doubles triangles to make one Combination quilt, you will have enough to make another. In the third part are quilts made using Sides triangles to show you how to use these little bonuses.

In the quilt project instructions, we present information to make the Doubles triangles first. These form the basis for each pair of Tops and Tails quilts or Combination quilts. Additional materials and instructions follow to make each quilt in the pair.

We do not, however, want you to be committed to making any pair of quilts because you like the look of just one of them. We encourage you to "mix and match" from the possibilities. You may like the look of the Tops quilt of one pair and the Tails quilt of another pair. With this in mind, we have written the instructions for each quilt with its own set of fabric requirements, so that you can make a particular quilt without having to make the second one of the pair. If you do want to make both quilts in a pair as shown, we have also listed the combined total fabric amounts needed to make both quilt tops and bindings. Look for the "Fabric Totals for Both Quilts" box.

Our aim is to help you take your own journey, to make quilts using your own choice of fabric and your own selection of quilt design. That's the exciting thing—finding out what is right for your ideas and your fabrics.

As for quilting, we chose to ditch quilt (that is, quilt along the seam lines) following the patterns of the piecing. We then added extra lines, sometimes straight and sometimes wavy, into spaces and borders. Often the piecing lines suggested the directions for the extra quilting lines. You may choose to quilt like this, or use overall free-motion machine quilting designs. The choice of quilting is up to you.

PLEASE NOTE:

- All fabric requirements are based on 42"-wide fabric, of which 40" is usable.

- All cutting measurements include ¼" seam allowances.

- Cut across the full width of the fabric unless otherwise specified.

- For quilt construction techniques, refer to "Quiltmaking Basics" (pages 88–95).

BEACH BROLLIES

Australians affectionately call umbrellas brollies. These two quilts remind us of striped beach umbrellas on the golden sand. The contrast between the two groups of fat quarters in these quilts is created with stripes and hand-dyed-style prints, a contrast mainly between the print styles. The accent color is red.

 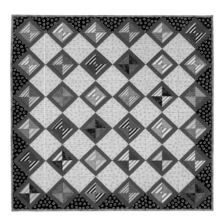

DOUBLES TRIANGLES

MATERIALS FOR THE DOUBLES TRIANGLES

- ⅝ yard *each* of 6 bright striped fabrics*

- 6 fat quarters of hand-dyed-style prints: 1 *each* of orange, blue, green, purple, pink, and dark pink

- 1⅞ yards of red solid for accent color

*Or 6 fat quarters. See "Using Stripes" (page 16).

MAKING THE DOUBLES TRIANGLES

Following the instructions (pages 15–19), make the Tops and Tails triangles. Note that the stripes should be parallel to the long edge of the strips.

BEACH BROLLIES: TOPS QUILT

Pieced and quilted by Judy Hooworth ～ Finished quilt: 56" x 56"

ADDITIONAL MATERIALS FOR TOPS QUILT

- 1⅝ yards of yellow print for second border
- ½ yard of black print for third border
- ⅜ yard of red solid for first border (2¼ yards *total* combined with accent fabric)
- ⅝ yard of orange tone-on-tone print for binding
- 3½ yards of fabric for backing
- 60" x 60" piece of batting

CUTTING

All measurements include ¼" seam allowances. Cut across the full width of the fabric unless otherwise specified.

From the red solid, cut:
5 strips, 2" wide

From the black print, cut:
6 strips, 2½" wide

From the yellow print, cut on the lengthwise grain:
4 strips, 5" wide

From the orange tone-on-tone print, cut:
6 strips, 3" wide

ASSEMBLING THE QUILT TOP

1. Using the Tops triangles, make 36 blocks, pairing the same combinations of prints together.

Make 36.

2. Arrange and sew the blocks together to make the quilt center as shown in the quilt diagram.

3. Cut one of the red strips in half. Sew each half strip to a full-length red strip.

4. Cut two of the black strips in half. Sew each half strip to a full-length black strip.

5. Using the red strips for the first border, the yellow strips for the second border, and the black strips for the third border, attach each border using the method for butted corners (page 91).

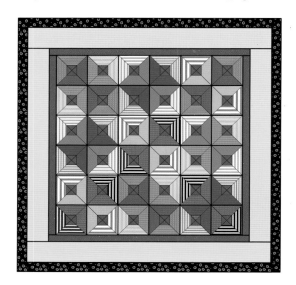

FINISHING THE QUILT

1. Cut and piece the backing fabric. Layer and baste the quilt top, batting, and backing.

2. Hand or machine quilt as desired.

3. Using the orange strips, prepare and sew the binding to the quilt.

BEACH BROLLIES: TAILS QUILT
Pieced and quilted by Judy Hooworth ❧ Finished quilt: 56½" x 56½"

ADDITIONAL MATERIALS FOR TAILS QUILT

- 1⅛ yards of yellow print for alternate blocks
- ⅔ yard of black print for setting triangles
- ⅝ yard of green tone-on-tone print for binding
- 3½ yards of fabric for backing
- 61" x 61" piece of batting

CUTTING

All measurements include ¼" seam allowances. Cut across the full width of the fabric unless otherwise specified.

From the yellow print, cut:
5 strips, 7" wide; crosscut into 25 squares, 7" x 7"

From the black print, cut:
2 strips, 10½" wide; crosscut into 5 squares, 10½" x 10½". Cut each square diagonally twice to make a total of 20 quarter-square triangles. Trim the remainder of the second strip to 5½" wide and cut 2 squares, 5½" x 5½". Cut each square in half diagonally to make 4 half-square triangles.

From the green tone-on-tone print, cut:
6 strips, 3" wide

ASSEMBLING THE QUILT TOP

1. Using the Tails triangles, make 36 blocks.

Make 36.

2. Arrange the Tails blocks, the yellow alternate blocks, and the black setting triangles to make the quilt center as shown in the quilt diagram. Sew all these together using a diagonal construction.

FINISHING THE QUILT

1. Cut and piece the backing fabric. Layer and baste the quilt top, batting, and backing.

2. Hand or machine quilt as desired.

3. Using the green strips, prepare and sew the binding to the quilt.

FABRIC TOTALS FOR BOTH QUILTS

If you plan to make both Beach Brollies projects, the yardage below is enough to make both quilt tops and bindings.

- ⅝ yard *each* of 6 bright striped fabrics*
- 6 fat quarters of hand-dyed-style prints, 1 *each* of orange, blue, green, purple, pink, and dark pink
- 2¼ yards of red solid
- 2¼ yards of yellow print
- 1⅛ yards of black print
- ⅝ yard of orange tone-on-tone print
- ⅝ yard of green tone-on-tone print

Or 6 fat quarters. See "Using Stripes" (page 16).

BUNTING

In these festive quilts, the contrast between the two groups of fat quarters is made with red prints and blue prints. Because all the blue prints have white backgrounds, they read as lighter than the red prints. Thus the contrast is created through color as well as value. The accent color is a bright blue.

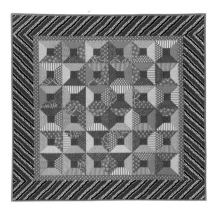 

DOUBLES TRIANGLES

MATERIALS FOR THE DOUBLES TRIANGLES

- 6 fat quarters of blue-and-white prints
- 6 fat quarters of red prints
- 1⅞ yards of bright blue solid for accent color

MAKING THE DOUBLES TRIANGLES

Following the instructions (pages 15–19), make the Tops and Tails triangles.

BUNTING: TOPS QUILT

Pieced and quilted by Judy Hooworth ~ Finished quilt: 55" x 55"

ADDITIONAL MATERIALS FOR TOPS QUILT

- 1⅔ yards of blue striped fabric for second border
- ⅜ yard of red print for first border
- ⅝ yard of red solid for binding
- 3½ yards of fabric for backing
- 59" x 59" piece of batting

CUTTING

All measurements include ¼" seam allowances. Cut across the full width of the fabric unless otherwise specified.

From the red print, cut:
5 strips, 2" wide

From the blue striped fabric, cut on the *lengthwise* **grain:**
4 strips, 6½" wide

From the red solid, cut:
6 strips, 3" wide

ASSEMBLING THE QUILT TOP

1. Using the Tops triangles, make 36 Tops blocks as shown.

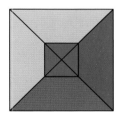

Make 36.

2. Arrange and sew the quilt blocks together to make the quilt center as shown in the quilt diagram.

3. Cut one of the 2"-wide red print strips in half. Sew each half strip to a full-length red print strip.

4. Using the red print strips for the first border and the blue striped strips for the second border, attach each border using the method for butted corners (page 91).

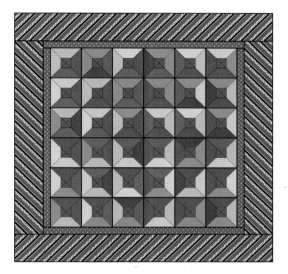

FINISHING THE QUILT

1. Cut and piece the backing fabric. Layer and baste the quilt top, batting, and backing.

2. Hand or machine quilt as desired.

3. Using the red solid strips, prepare and sew the binding to the quilt.

BUNTING: TAILS QUILT

Pieced and quilted by Judy Hooworth ～ Finished quilt: 61½" x 61½"

ADDITIONAL MATERIALS FOR TAILS QUILT

- 1¾ yards of white tone-on-tone print for Pinwheel blocks and borders*

- 1 yard of white-and-red polka-dot print for setting triangles

- ⅝ yard of light blue print for alternate blocks

- ⅔ yard of blue print for binding

- 4 yards of fabric for backing

- 66" x 66" piece of batting

When Judy made this quilt, she ran out of white tone-on-tone fabric used in the Pinwheel blocks and had to substitute a different fabric in the borders. The directions are written using just one fabric, as originally intended. Also note that the directions include a simpler method of piecing the border corners.

CUTTING

All measurements include ¼" seam allowances. Cut across the full width of the fabric unless otherwise specified.

From the white tone-on-tone print, cut:
8 strips, 5½" wide; crosscut into 50 squares, 5½" x 5½". Cut each square in half diagonally to make 100 half-square triangles.
7 strips, 1½" wide

From the light blue print, cut:
3 strips, 5½" wide; crosscut into 18 squares, 5½" x 5½". Cut each square in half diagonally to make 36 half-square triangles.

From the white-and-red polka-dot print, cut:
2 strips, 14¼" wide; crosscut into 3 squares, 14¼" x 14¼". Cut each square diagonally twice to make 12 quarter-square triangles. Trim the remainder of the second strip to 7⅜" wide; crosscut into 2 squares, 7⅜" x 7⅜". Cut each square in half diagonally to make 4 half-square triangles.

From the blue print for binding, cut:
7 strips, 3" wide

ASSEMBLING THE QUILT TOP

1. Using the red Tails triangles, make 64 units combining one Tails triangle with one white print triangle.

Make 64.

2. Make 16 blocks using the units from step 1.

Make 16.

3. Using the blue Tails triangles, make 36 units combining one Tails triangle with one light blue triangle.

Make 36.

4. Using the 36 units from step 3, make nine blocks.

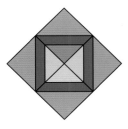

Make 9.

5. Arrange the pieced blocks and the white-and-red polka-dot setting triangles to make the quilt center as shown in the quilt diagram. Sew all these together using a diagonal construction.

6. Using the remaining white triangles and blue Tails triangles, sew eight Tails triangles to nine white triangles to make the pieced border. Repeat to make four border strips.

Make 4.

7. Sew the pieced border to the quilt, using the method for mitered corners (page 91).

8. Sew four of the white strips together into pairs.

9. Cut one of the three remaining white strips in half. Sew each half strip to a full-length white strip.

10. Sew the white borders to the quilt using the method for butted corners (page 91).

FINISHING THE QUILT

1. Cut and piece the backing fabric. Layer and baste the quilt top, batting, and backing.

2. Hand or machine quilt as desired.

3. Using the blue strips, prepare and sew the binding to the quilt.

FABRIC TOTALS FOR BOTH QUILTS

If you plan to make both Bunting projects, the yardage below is enough to make both quilt tops and bindings.

- 6 fat quarters of blue-and-white prints
- 6 fat quarters of red prints
- 1⅞ yards of bright blue solid
- 1¾ yards of white tone-on-tone print
- 1⅔ yards of blue striped fabric
- 1 yard of white-and-red polka-dot print
- ⅝ yard of red solid
- ⅔ yard of blue print
- ⅜ yard of red print

CARNIVAL

Bright stripes and polka dots make for a happy-go-lucky pair of quilts. The contrast between the two groups of fat quarters is created with striped fabrics and hand-dyed-style prints. Thus the contrast is mainly between the print styles. The accent color is one of our favorites—red.

 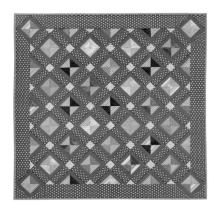

DOUBLES TRIANGLES

MATERIALS FOR THE DOUBLES TRIANGLES

- ⅝ yard *each* of 6 bright striped fabrics*

- 6 fat quarters of hand-dyed-style prints, 1 *each* of orange, yellow, purple, pink, green, and dark green (or colors to coordinate with the stripes)

- 1⅞ yards of red solid for accent color

Or 6 fat quarters. See "Using Stripes" (page 16).

MAKING THE DOUBLES TRIANGLES

Following the instructions (pages 15–19), make the Tops and Tails triangles. Note that the stripes should be parallel to the long edge of the strips.

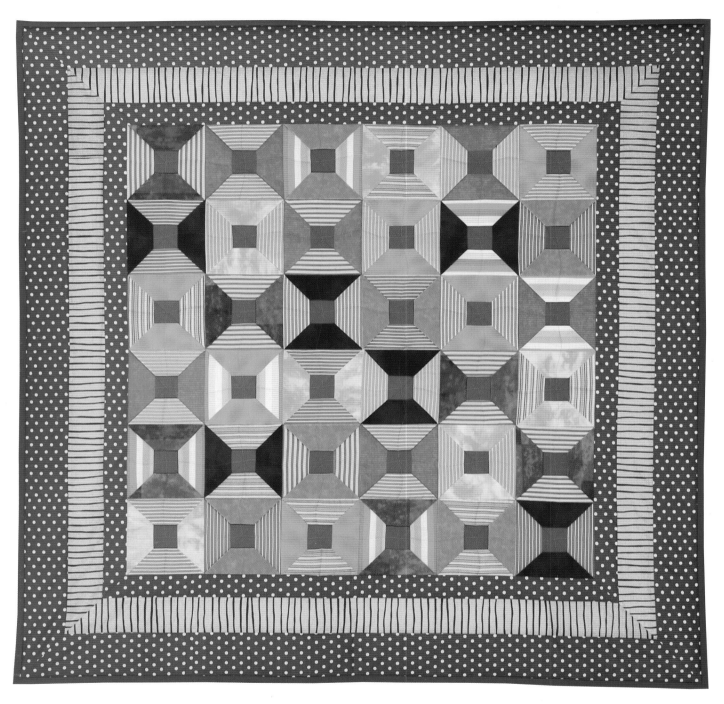

CARNIVAL: TOPS QUILT

Pieced and quilted by Judy Hooworth ∼ Finished quilt: 58" x 58"

ADDITIONAL MATERIALS FOR TOPS QUILT

- 1⅞ yards of purple polka-dot print for first and third borders
- ⅔ yard of yellow striped fabric for second border
- ⅔ yard of turquoise solid for binding
- 3½ yards of fabric for backing
- 62" x 62" piece of batting

CUTTING

All measurements include ¼" seam allowances. Cut across the full width of the fabric unless otherwise specified.

From the purple polka-dot print, cut on the lengthwise grain:
4 strips, 2½" wide
4 strips, 4½" wide

From the yellow striped fabric, cut:
6 strips, 3½" wide

From the turquoise solid, cut:
7 strips, 3" wide

ASSEMBLING THE QUILT TOP

1. Using the Tops triangles, make 36 blocks.

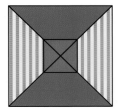

Make 36.

2. Arrange and sew the blocks together to make the quilt center.

3. Cut two of the yellow striped strips in half. Sew each half strip to a full-length yellow striped strip.

4. Using the narrower purple polka-dot strips for the first border, the yellow striped strips for the second border, and the wider purple polka-dot strips for the third border, sew the borders to the quilt using the method for mitered corners (page 91).

FINISHING THE QUILT

1. Cut and piece the backing fabric. Layer and baste the quilt top, batting, and backing.

2. Hand or machine quilt as desired.

3. Using the turquoise strips, prepare and sew the binding to the quilt.

FABRIC TOTALS FOR BOTH QUILTS

If you plan to make both Carnival projects, the yardage below is enough to make both quilt tops and bindings.

- ⅝ yard *each* of 6 bright striped fabrics*
- 6 fat quarters of hand-dyed-style prints, 1 *each* of orange, yellow, purple, pink, green, and dark green
- 1⅞ yards of red solid
- 3⅝ yards of purple polka-dot print
- ⅔ yard of yellow striped fabric
- ⅔ yard of turquoise solid
- ⅔ yard of green solid
- ⅓ yard of yellow print

*Or 6 fat quarters. See "Using Stripes" (page 16).

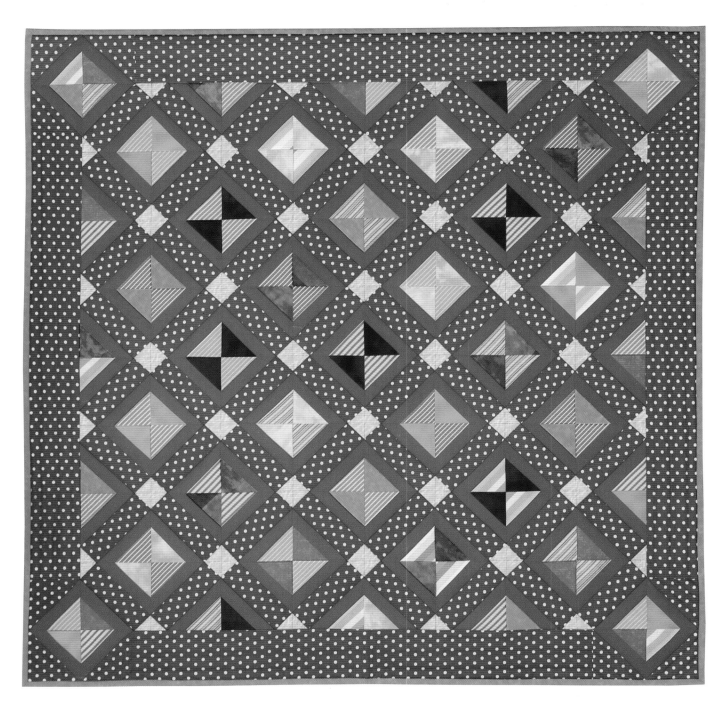

CARNIVAL: TAILS QUILT

Pieced and quilted by Judy Hooworth ∽ Finished quilt: 58¾" x 58¾"

ADDITIONAL MATERIALS FOR TAILS QUILT

- ⁓ 1⅞ yards of purple polka-dot print for sashing and border
- ⁓ ⅓ yard of yellow print for sashing cornerstones
- ⁓ ⅔ yard of green solid for binding
- ⁓ 3⅝ yards of fabric for backing
- ⁓ 63" x 63" piece of batting

CUTTING

All measurements include ¼" seam allowances. Cut across the full width of the fabric unless otherwise specified.

From the purple polka-dot print, cut:
13 strips, 2½" wide; crosscut into 64 rectangles, 2½" x 7"
4 strips, 5⅛" wide; trim each strip to a length of 39¾"
1 strip, 5½" wide; crosscut into 6 squares, 5½" x 5½". Cut each square in half diagonally to make 12 half-square triangles.

From the yellow print, cut:
3 strips, 2½" wide; crosscut into 40 squares, 2½" x 2½"

From the green solid, cut:
7 strips, 3" wide

ASSEMBLING THE QUILT TOP

1. It is easiest to make this quilt if first you use your design wall to lay out all the Tails triangles, sashing strips, and cornerstones, including the triangles for the four Tails blocks in the border.

2. Piece together the 25 Tails blocks for the quilt center, and 6 half blocks and 6 reverse half blocks for the sides of the quilt. *Do not sew the Tails triangles of the four corner blocks yet—these must be left unsewn at this point.* One triangle from each corner will be incorporated into the center of the quilt, while the other

triangles of these four blocks will be sewn into the border later.

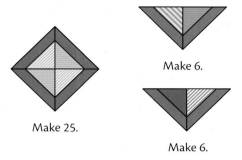

Make 25.

Make 6.

Make 6.

3. Arrange the blocks, sashing strips, yellow sashing cornerstones, and the four Tails triangles for the corners. Sew the quilt center together in diagonal rows. Note that the yellow cornerstones will extend beyond the edges. Trim the yellow squares even with the edges of the quilt.

4. Sew the purple polka-dot half-square triangles to the remaining Tails triangles for the corners.

Make 6.   Make 6.

5. Keeping the position of the Tails units correct, sew a Tails unit to each end of two purple strips. Sew these pieced strips to each side of the quilt center.

6. Again keeping the position of the Tails units correct, piece the top and bottom border strips to the remaining units of Tails triangles. Sew the top and bottom border strips to the quilt center.

FINISHING THE QUILT

1. Cut and piece the backing fabric. Layer and baste the quilt top, batting, and backing.

2. Hand or machine quilt as desired.

3. Using the green strips, prepare and sew the binding to the quilt.

CRIMSON CRANES

This pair of quilts can be designed using a great border fabric as the starting point, such as the lovely black-red-and-white crane print used here. The contrast between the two groups of fat eighths in these quilts is made with red prints and black prints, creating a contrast in both color and value. The accent color is a light beige.

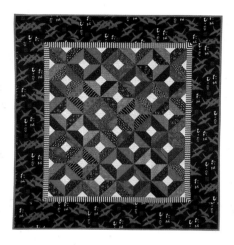 

DOUBLES TRIANGLES

MATERIALS FOR THE DOUBLES TRIANGLES

- 12 fat eighths of red prints

- 12 fat eighths of black prints

- 1⅞ yards of beige tone-on-tone print for accent color

MAKING THE DOUBLES TRIANGLES

Following the instructions (pages 15–19), make the Tops and Tails triangles.

CRIMSON CRANES: TOPS QUILT

Pieced and quilted by Margaret Rolfe ~ Finished quilt: 56" x 60⅝"

ADDITIONAL MATERIALS FOR TOPS QUILT

- 2 yards of black-and-red print for second border*

- ⅜ yard of black-and-white striped fabric for first border

- ⅔ yard of red tone-on-tone print for binding

- 3½ yards of fabric for backing

- 60" x 65" piece of batting

Note that in the quilt shown, the crane print used for the second border was a one-way directional print, and the borders were added using the method for butted corners. The two side border strips were cut lengthwise; the top and bottom border strips were made from strips cut across the remaining width of the fabric, with joins making the lengths required. The instructions here are written for mitered borders to match the mitered striped border.

CUTTING

All measurements include ¼" seam allowances. Cut across the full width of the fabric unless otherwise specified.

From the black-and-white striped fabric, cut:
5 strips, 2" wide

From the black-and-red print, cut on the *lengthwise* grain:
4 strips, 8" wide

From the red tone-on-tone print, cut:
7 strips, 3" wide

ASSEMBLING THE QUILT TOP

1. Using the Tops triangles, make 28 blocks, 12 half blocks with the red print on the left, and 3 half blocks with the red print on the right. Pair the same combinations of prints together in the blocks.

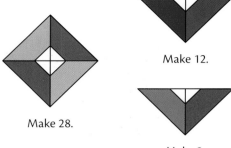

Make 28.

Make 12.

Make 3.

2. Arrange the blocks, half blocks, and remaining two triangles to make the quilt center as shown in the quilt diagram. Sew all these together, using a diagonal construction.

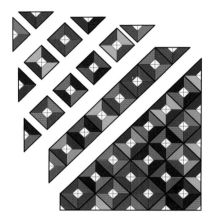

3. Cut one strip of the black-and-white striped fabric into four equal pieces. Sew one of these pieces to each of the remaining four strips, carefully matching the stripes.

4. Using the black-and-white striped fabric for the first border and the black-and-red print for the second border, attach the borders to the quilt, using the method for mitered corners (page 91).

FINISHING THE QUILT

1. Cut and piece the backing fabric. Layer and baste the quilt top, batting, and backing.

2. Hand or machine quilt as desired.

3. Using the red tone-on-tone strips, prepare and sew the binding to the quilt.

CRIMSON CRANES: TAILS QUILT
Pieced and quilted by Margaret Rolfe ～ Finished quilt: 55" x 55"

ADDITIONAL MATERIALS FOR TAILS QUILT

- 1¾ yards of black-and-red print for border*
- ⅝ yard of red tone-on-tone print for binding
- 3½ yards of fabric for backing
- 59" x 59" piece of batting

CUTTING

All measurements include ¼" seam allowances. Cut across the full width of the fabric unless otherwise specified.

From the black-and-red print, cut on the *lengthwise* grain:
4 strips, 8" wide (for mitered corners)*

From the red tone-on-tone print, cut:
6 strips, 3" wide

* For a one-way directional print fabric, add the borders using the method for butted corners. Cut 2 strips, 8" wide across the width of the fabric. Then cut 2 strips, 8" wide, lengthwise. Cut 2 additional strips, 8" wide, across the remaining width of fabric; join these strips to the other crosswise strips, matching the pattern as best you can.

ASSEMBLING THE QUILT TOP

1. Arrange the Tails triangles to make the quilt design as shown in the quilt diagram. Sew pairs of triangles together to make 60 blocks.

Make 60.

2. Sew blocks and side triangles together using a diagonal construction.

3. Sew the black-and-red print strips to the quilt center using the method for mitered corners (page 91), or butted corners if you prefer (page 91).

FINISHING THE QUILT

1. Cut and piece the backing fabric. Layer and baste the quilt top, batting, and backing.

2. Hand or machine quilt as desired.

3. Using the red print strips, prepare and sew the binding to the quilt.

FABRIC TOTALS FOR BOTH QUILTS

If you plan to make both Crimson Cranes projects, the yardage below is enough to make both quilt tops and bindings.

- 12 fat eighths of red prints
- 12 fat eighths of black prints
- 1⅞ yards of beige tone-on-tone print
- 3⅝ yards of black-and-red print
- 1¼ yards of red tone-on-tone print
- ⅜ yard of black-and-white striped fabric

FALLING WATER

The blues and aquas of these quilts bring to mind waterfalls and rain— always welcome in our country. Prints in light greens and aquas are combined with darker blue prints, making a contrast between light and dark values. The accent color is red.

 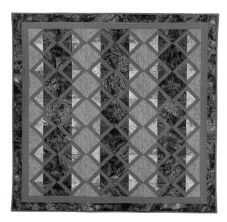

DOUBLES TRIANGLES

MATERIALS FOR THE DOUBLES TRIANGLES

- ~ 6 fat quarters of prints in light greens and aquas

- ~ 6 fat quarters of blue prints

- ~ 1⅞ yards of red solid for accent color

MAKING THE DOUBLES TRIANGLES

Following the instructions (pages 15–19), make the Tops and Tails triangles.

FALLING WATER: TOPS QUILT
Pieced and quilted by Judy Hooworth ❧ Finished quilt: 56" x 56"

ADDITIONAL MATERIALS FOR TOPS QUILT

- 1¾ yards of blue batik for third border

- ¾ yard of red solid for second border and binding (2⅝ yards *total* combined with accent fabric)

- ⅜ yard of aqua print for first border

- 3½ yards of fabric for backing

- 60" x 60" piece of batting

CUTTING

All measurements include ¼" seam allowances. Cut across the full width of the fabric unless otherwise specified.

From the aqua print, cut:
5 strips, 2" wide

From the red solid, cut:
5 strips, 1" wide
6 strips, 3" wide

From the blue batik, cut on the *lengthwise* grain:
4 strips, 6½" wide

ASSEMBLING THE QUILT TOP

1. Using the Tops triangles, make 36 blocks.

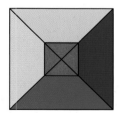

Make 36.

2. Arrange and sew the blocks together to make the quilt center as shown in the quilt photo.

3. Cut one of the aqua strips in half. Sew each half strip to a full-length aqua strip.

4. Cut one of the 1"-wide red strips into four equal pieces. Sew each quarter strip to a full-length 1"-wide red strip.

5. Using the aqua strips for the first border, the 1"-wide red strips for the second border, and the blue batik strips for the third border, attach each border to the quilt using the method for butted corners (page 91).

FINISHING THE QUILT

1. Cut and piece the backing fabric. Layer and baste the quilt top, batting, and backing.

2. Hand or machine quilt as desired.

3. Using the red strips, prepare and sew the binding to the quilt.

FABRIC TOTALS FOR BOTH QUILTS

If you plan to make both Falling Water projects, the yardage below is enough to make both quilt tops and bindings.

- 6 fat quarters of light green and aqua prints

- 6 fat quarters of blue prints

- 3⅜ yards of red solid

- 3½ yards of blue batik

- 1⅜ yards of aqua print

- ¾ yard of blue solid

FALLING WATER: TAILS QUILT
Pieced and quilted by Judy Hooworth ～ Finished quilt: 67½" x 67½"

ADDITIONAL MATERIALS FOR TAILS QUILT

- 2 yards of blue batik for alternate blocks, setting triangles, and second border

- 1⅛ yards of aqua print for alternate blocks and setting triangles

- ¾ yard of blue solid for first border

- ⅞ yard of red solid for binding

- 4¼ yards of fabric for backing

- 72" x 72" piece of batting

CUTTING

All measurements include ¼" seam allowances. Cut across the full width of the fabric unless otherwise specified.

From the blue batik, cut:
3 strips, 7" wide; crosscut into 15 squares, 7" x 7"
1 strip, 10½" wide; crosscut into 2 squares, 10½" x 10½". Cut each square diagonally twice to make a total of 8 quarter-square triangles; 2 are extra.
8 strips, 3¾" wide

From the aqua print, cut:
2 strips, 7" wide; crosscut into 10 squares, 7" x 7"
2 strips, 10½" wide; crosscut into 4 squares, 10½" x 10½". Cut each square diagonally twice to make a total of 16 quarter-square triangles; 2 are extra.
Trim the remainder of the second strip to 5½" wide and crosscut into 2 squares, 5½" x 5½". Cut each square in half diagonally to make a total of 4 half-square triangles.

From the blue solid, cut:
8 strips, 2¾" wide

From the red solid, cut:
8 strips, 3" wide

ASSEMBLING THE QUILT TOP

1. Using the Tails triangles, make 36 blocks.

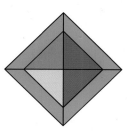

Make 36.

2. Arrange the Tails blocks, blue batik alternate blocks, aqua alternate blocks, and all the side and corner triangles to make the quilt center as shown in the quilt diagram. Sew all these together, using a diagonal construction.

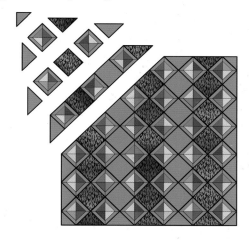

3. Sew the blue solid strips together into pairs.

4. Sew the blue batik strips together into pairs.

5. Using the blue solid strips for the first border and the blue batik strips for the second border, attach each border to the quilt center, using the method for butted corners (page 91).

FINISHING THE QUILT

1. Cut and piece the backing fabric. Layer and baste the quilt top, batting, and backing.

2. Hand or machine quilt as desired.

3. Using the red strips, prepare and sew the binding to the quilt.

SOUTH PACIFIC

The tropical black-and-white prints, paired with warm oranges and cool blue, will have you dreaming of a favorite island in no time. The contrast in the two groups of fat eighths is between the black-and-white prints and orange prints, thus creating contrast through both color and value. The accent color is blue.

 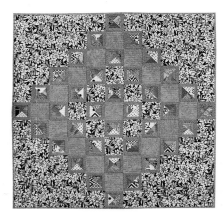

DOUBLES TRIANGLES

MATERIALS FOR THE DOUBLES TRIANGLES

- 12 fat eighths of black-and-white prints
- 12 fat eighths of orange prints
- 1⅞ yards of blue print for accent color

MAKING THE DOUBLES TRIANGLES

Following the instructions (pages 15–19), make the Tops and Tails triangles.

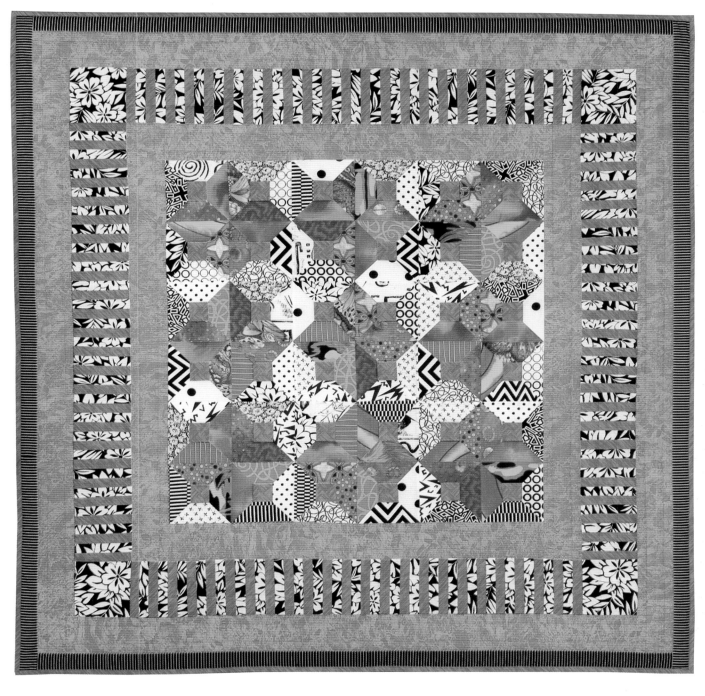

SOUTH PACIFIC: TOPS QUILT
Pieced and quilted by Judy Hooworth ~ Finished quilt: 72" x 72"

ADDITIONAL MATERIALS FOR TOPS QUILT

- 1⅔ yards of orange print for first and third borders

- 1½ yards of blue print for pieced second border and binding (3⅜ yards *total* combined with accent fabric)

- 1 yard of black-and-white print for pieced second border

- ⅔ yard of black-and-white striped fabric for fourth border

- 4½ yards of fabric for backing

- 76" x 76" piece of batting

CUTTING

All measurements include ¼" seam allowances. Cut across the full width of the fabric unless otherwise specified.

From the black-and-white print, cut:
1 strip, 6½" wide; crosscut into 4 squares,
   6½" x 6½"
16 strips, 1½" wide

From the blue print, cut:
16 strips, 1½" wide
8 strips, 3" wide

From the orange print, cut:
12 strips, 4½" wide

From the black-and-white striped fabric, cut:
8 strips, 2½" wide

ASSEMBLING THE QUILT TOP

1. Using the Tops triangles, make 36 blocks.

Make 36.

2. Arrange and sew the blocks together to make the quilt center as shown in the quilt diagram.

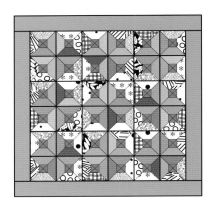

MAKING AND ADDING THE BORDERS

1. Sew the 1½"-wide black-and-white print strips to the 1½"-wide blue strips in groups of eight strips, alternating the two colors. Sew each strip in the opposite direction of the previous strip to prevent the strip sets from curving.

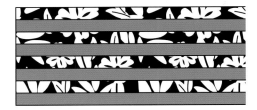

Make 4.

2. Crosscut each of the four strip sets into 6 segments, 6½" wide, to make a total of 24 segments.

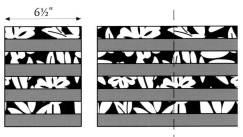

6½"

Cut 24 segments.

3. From four of the segments, remove one black-and-white print strip from the outside edge.

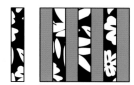

Make 4.

4. Sew five full segments and one partial segment together to make one pieced border strip. Repeat to make a total of four pieced border strips.

5. Sew one 6½" black-and-white print square to

Make 4.

each end of two of the pieced strips.

6. Cut two of the orange strips in half. Sew each

Make 2.

half strip to a full-length orange strip.

7. Join four of the orange strips together into pairs.

8. Join the eight black-and-white striped strips together into pairs.

9. Using the shorter orange strips for the first

border, the pieced strips for the second border, the longer orange strips for the third border, and the black-and-white striped strips for the fourth border, attach the borders using the method for butted corners (page 91).

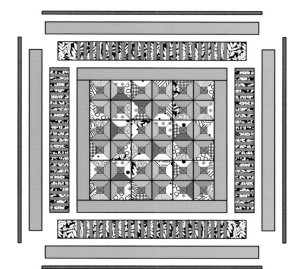

FINISHING THE QUILT

1. Cut and piece the backing fabric. Layer and baste the quilt top, batting, and backing.

2. Hand or machine quilt as desired.

3. Using the blue strips, prepare and sew the binding to the quilt.

FABRIC TOTALS FOR BOTH QUILTS

If you plan to make both South Pacific projects, the yardage below is enough to make both quilt tops and bindings.

- 12 fat eighths of black-and-white prints
- 12 fat eighths of orange prints
- 3⅜ yards of blue print
- 3¾ yards of black-and-white print
- 3¼ yards of orange print
- ⅔ yard of black-and-white striped fabric

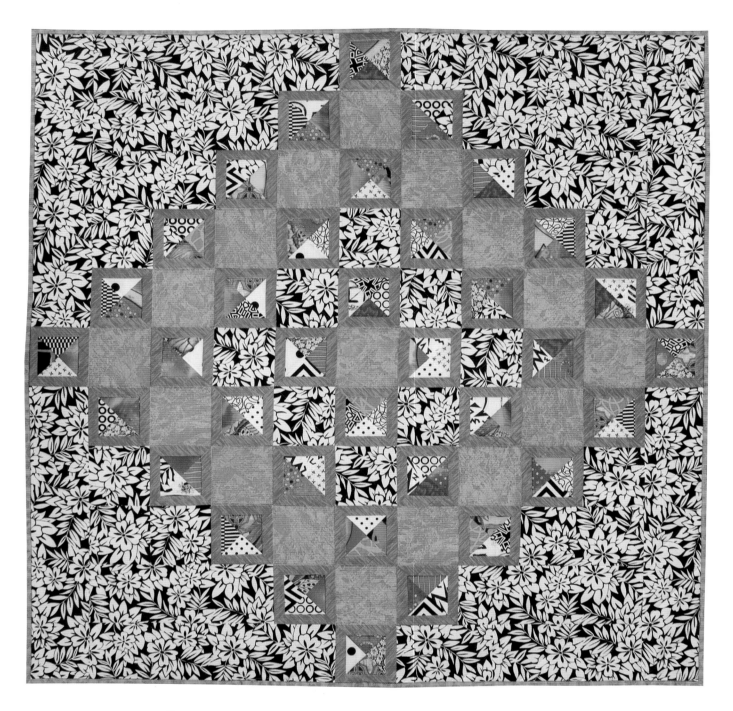

SOUTH PACIFIC: TAILS QUILT

Pieced and quilted by Judy Hooworth ∼ Finished quilt: 72½" x 72½"

ADDITIONAL MATERIALS FOR TAILS QUILT

- 2⅞ yards of black-and-white print for alternate blocks and background
- 1⅝ yards of orange print for alternate blocks and binding
- 4½ yards of fabric for backing
- 77" x 77" piece of batting

CUTTING

All measurements include ¼" seam allowances. Cut across the full width of the fabric unless otherwise specified.

From the orange print, cut:
4 strips, 7" wide; crosscut into 17 squares, 7" x 7"
8 strips, 3" wide

From the black-and-white print, cut:
13 strips, 7" wide; crosscut into the following:
    From 4 strips, cut 4 strips, 7" x 33" (D)
    From 4 strips, cut 4 strips, 7" x 26½" (C)
    From 2 strips, cut 4 strips, 7" x 20" (B)
    From 2 strips, cut 4 strips, 7" x 13½" (A)
    From leftover pieces, cut 12 squares, 7" x 7"

ASSEMBLING THE QUILT TOP

1. Using the Tails triangles, make 36 blocks as shown.

Make 4.

Make 4.

Make 24.

Make 4.

2. Arrange the Tails blocks, orange squares, black-and-white squares, and the A, B, and C strips as shown in the quilt diagram.

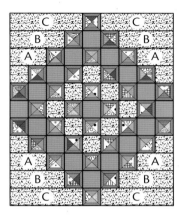

3. Sew the horizontal rows to make the quilt center. Sew the rows together.

4. Sew the D strips and remaining blocks together and sew these to opposite sides of the quilt center.

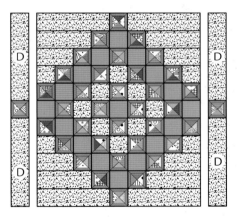

FINISHING THE QUILT

1. Cut and piece the backing fabric. Layer and baste the quilt top, batting, and backing.

2. Hand or machine quilt as desired.

3. Using the orange strips, prepare and sew the binding to the quilt.

SUNNY PROVENCE

These quilts provide a change of scenery, transporting you to the south of France. The contrast in the two groups of fat quarters is between yellow prints and blue prints, creating a contrast in color as well as value. The accent color is orange.

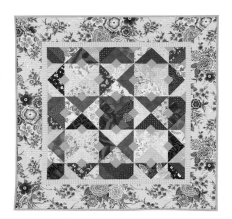 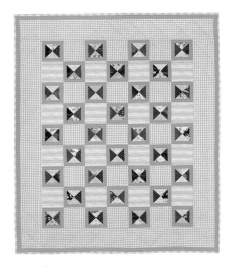

DOUBLES TRIANGLES

MATERIALS FOR THE DOUBLES TRIANGLES

- 6 fat quarters of yellow prints

- 6 fat quarters of blue prints

- 1⅞ yards of orange solid for accent color

MAKING THE DOUBLES TRIANGLES

Following the instructions (pages 15–19), make the Tops and Tails triangles.

SUNNY PROVENCE: TOPS QUILT

Pieced and quilted by Judy Hooworth ❧ Finished quilt: 55" x 55"

ADDITIONAL MATERIALS FOR TOPS QUILT

- 1⅞ yards of yellow-and-blue floral for second border

- ⅝ yard of orange solid for binding (2½ yards *total* combined with accent fabric)

- ⅜ yard of yellow striped fabric for first border

- 3½ yards of fabric for backing

- 59" x 59" piece of batting

CUTTING

All measurements include ¼" seam allowances. Cut across the full width of the fabric unless otherwise specified.

From the yellow striped fabric, cut:
5 strips, 2" wide

From the yellow-and-blue floral, cut on the *lengthwise* grain:
4 strips, 7½" wide

From the orange solid, cut:
6 strips, 3" wide

ASSEMBLING THE QUILT TOP

1. Using the Tops triangles, make 24 blocks, 8 half blocks with the yellow print on the left, and 8 half blocks with the yellow print on the right. There will be 16 triangles left over.

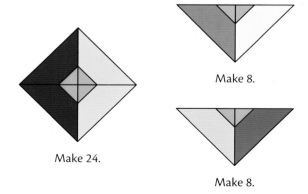

Make 24.

Make 8.

Make 8.

2. Arrange the blocks and half blocks to make the quilt center as shown. Sew all these together, using a diagonal construction.

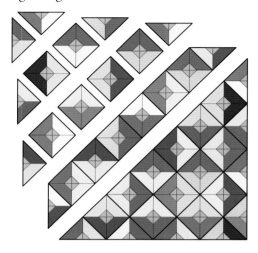

3. Cut one strip of yellow striped fabric into four equal pieces. Sew one of these pieces to each of the remaining four strips, carefully matching the stripes.

4. Using the yellow striped fabric for the first border and the yellow-and-blue floral for the second border, attach the borders to the quilt using the method for mitered corners (page 91).

FINISHING THE QUILT

1. Cut and piece the backing fabric. Layer and baste the quilt top, batting, and backing.

2. Hand or machine quilt as desired.

3. Using the orange strips, prepare and sew the binding to the quilt.

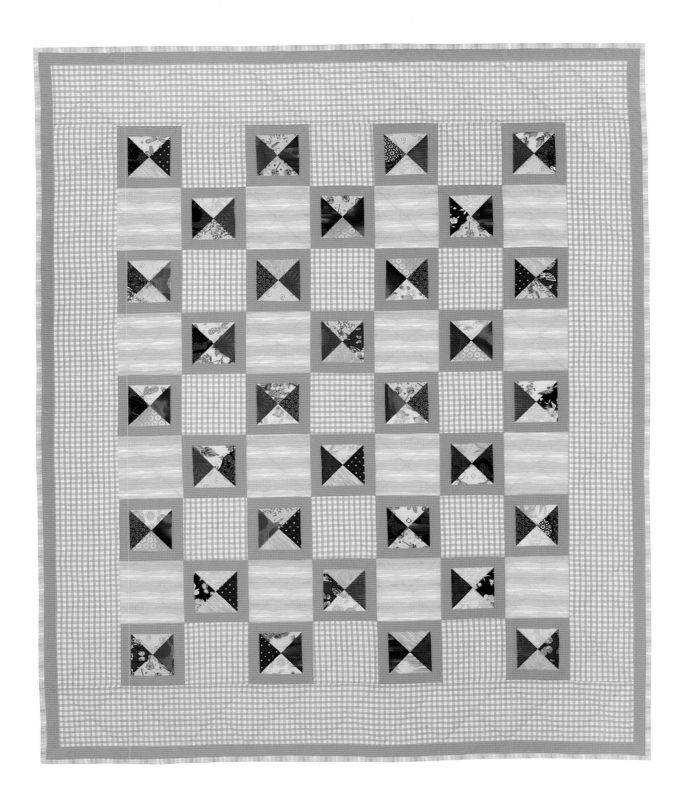

SUNNY PROVENCE: TAILS QUILT
Pieced and quilted by Judy Hooworth ～ **Finished quilt: 62" x 75"**

ADDITIONAL MATERIALS FOR TAILS QUILT

- 2¼ yards of orange gingham for alternate blocks and first border
- 1⅝ yards of yellow print for alternate blocks and binding
- ½ yard of orange solid for second border (2⅜ yards *total* combined with accent fabric)
- 4 yards of fabric for backing
- 66" x 79" piece of batting

CUTTING

All measurements include ¼" seam allowances. Cut across the full width of the fabric unless otherwise specified.

From the orange gingham, cut:
2 strips, 7" wide; crosscut into 10 squares, 7" x 7"
5 strips, 7" wide, from the *lengthwise* grain. Reserve 4 strips for the first border. Crosscut the remaining strip into 5 squares, 7" x 7".

From the yellow print, cut:
4 strips, 7" wide; crosscut into 16 squares, 7" x 7"
8 strips, 3" wide

From the orange solid, cut:
8 strips, 1¾" wide

ASSEMBLING THE QUILT TOP

1. Using the Tails triangles, make 32 blocks. You'll have 16 extra triangles.

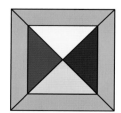

Make 32.

2. Arrange and sew the pieced blocks and the alternate blocks together to make the quilt center as shown in the quilt photo on page 59.

3. Sew the orange solid strips together into pairs.

4. Using the orange gingham for the first border and the orange solid for the second border, attach each border to the quilt center using the method for butted corners (page 91).

FINISHING

1. Cut and piece the backing fabric. Layer and baste the quilt top, batting, and backing.

2. Hand or machine quilt as desired.

3. Using the yellow strips, prepare and sew the binding to the quilt.

FABRIC TOTALS FOR BOTH QUILTS

If you plan to make both Sunny Provence projects, the yardage below is enough to make both quilt tops and bindings.

- 6 fat quarters of yellow prints
- 6 fat quarters of blue prints
- 3 yards of orange solid
- 2¼ yards of orange gingham
- 1⅞ yards of yellow-and-blue floral
- 1⅝ yards of yellow print
- ⅜ yard of yellow striped fabric

SUNNY-SIDE UP

The words bright and fun sum up this pair of quilts. The contrast between the two groups of fabric is created with bright striped fabrics and a variety of solid colors. Thus the contrast is mainly between print styles. The accent color is lime green.

 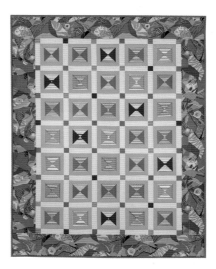

DOUBLES TRIANGLES

MATERIALS FOR THE DOUBLES TRIANGLES

- 6 pieces, *each* ⅝ yard*, of bright striped fabrics

- 6 pieces, *each* ¼ yard, of bright solids in red, orange, green, royal blue, blue, and pink

- 1⅞ yards of lime green solid for accent color

Or 6 fat quarters; see "Using Stripes" (page 16).

MAKING THE DOUBLES TRIANGLES

Following the instructions (pages 15–19), make the Tops and Tails triangles. Note that the stripes are parallel to the strips.

SUNNY-SIDE UP: TOPS QUILT
Pieced and quilted by Margaret Rolfe ～ Finished quilt: 56" x 56"

ADDITIONAL MATERIALS FOR TOPS QUILT

- 1⅞ yards of bright print for second border
- ⅜ yard of lime green solid for first border (2¼ yards *total* combined with the accent fabric)
- ⅝ yard of red solid for binding
- 3½ yards of fabric for backing
- 60" x 60" piece of batting

CUTTING

All measurements include ¼" seam allowances. Cut across the full width of the fabric unless otherwise specified.

From the lime green solid, cut:
5 strips, 2" wide

From the bright print, cut on the *lengthwise* grain:
4 strips, 7" wide

From the red solid, cut:
6 strips, 3" wide

ASSEMBLING THE QUILT TOP

1. Using the Tops triangles, make 36 blocks, 18 using the striped fabrics and 18 using the solids, with the same fabrics within each block.

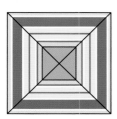
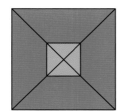

Make 18.   Make 18.

2. Arrange and sew the blocks together to make the quilt center as shown in the quilt diagram.

3. Cut one of the lime green strips into four equal pieces. Sew each quarter strip to a full-length lime green strip.

4. Using the lime green strips for the first border and the bright print strips for the second border, sew the borders to the quilt using the method for mitered corners (page 91).

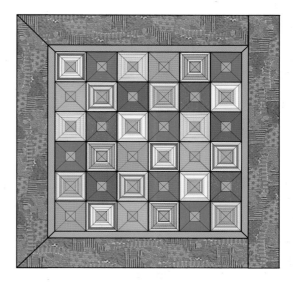

FINISHING THE QUILT

1. Cut and piece the backing fabric. Layer and baste the quilt top, batting, and backing.

2. Hand or machine quilt as desired.

3. Using the red strips, prepare and sew the binding to the quilt.

SUNNY-SIDE UP: TAILS QUILT
Pieced and quilted by Margaret Rolfe ~ Finished quilt: 55½" x 71½"

ADDITIONAL MATERIALS FOR TAILS QUILT

- 1⅞ yards of bright print for border

- 1⅛ yards of yellow solid for sashing

- ⅛ yard *each* of 6 bright solids for sashing cornerstones (⅓ yard total *each* combined with fabric for the Doubles triangles)

- ⅔ yard of red solid for binding

- 3½ yards of fabric for backing

- 60" x 76" piece of batting

CUTTING

All measurements include ¼" seam allowances. Cut across the full width of the fabric unless otherwise specified.

From the yellow solid, cut:
17 strips, 2" wide; crosscut into 82 strips, 2" x 7"

From *each* of the 6 bright solids, cut:
1 strip, 2" wide; crosscut into 8 squares, 2" x 2" (48 squares total)

From the bright print, cut on the *lengthwise* grain:
4 strips, 7" wide

From the red solid, cut:
7 strips, 3" wide

ASSEMBLING THE QUILT TOP

1. Using the Tails triangles, make 35 blocks, pairing the same combinations of prints together. You'll have four extra triangles.

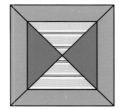

Make 35.

2. Arrange and sew the Tails blocks, sashing strips, and sashing cornerstones together to make the quilt center as shown in the quilt photo.

3. Using the bright print strips, sew the border to the quilt using the method for butted corners (page 91).

FINISHING THE QUILT

1. Cut and piece the backing fabric. Layer and baste the quilt top, batting, and backing.

2. Hand or machine quilt as desired.

3. Using the red strips, prepare and sew the binding to the quilt.

FABRIC TOTALS FOR BOTH QUILTS

If you plan to make both Sunny-Side Up projects, the yardage below is enough to make both quilt tops and bindings.

- 6 pieces, *each* ⅝ yard, of bright striped fabrics*

- 6 pieces, *each* ⅓ yard, of bright solids in red, orange, green, royal blue, blue, and pink

- 2¼ yards of lime green solid

- 1⅞ yards of bright print

- 1⅞ yards of a second bright print

- 1⅛ yards of yellow solid

- 1¼ yards of red solid

Or 6 fat quarters; see "Using Stripes" (page 16).

VAUDEVILLE

A wide variety of vibrant fabrics makes two strikingly different quilts. The contrast in the two groups of fat eighths is between bright striped fabrics and a variety of black prints with bold motifs. Thus the contrast is created with both print style and value. The accent color is red.

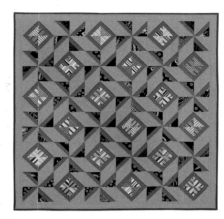

DOUBLES TRIANGLES

MATERIALS FOR THE DOUBLES TRIANGLES

- 12 fat eighths of bright striped fabrics*
- 12 fat eighths of black prints
- 1⅞ yards of red solid for accent color

Stripes should go lengthwise down fabric; see "Using Stripes" (page 16).

MAKING THE DOUBLES TRIANGLES

Following the instructions (pages 15–19), make the Tops and Tails triangles. Note that the stripes are perpendicular to the strips.

VAUDEVILLE: TOPS QUILT

Pieced and quilted by Judy Hooworth ∼ Finished quilt: 60½" x 60½"

ADDITIONAL MATERIALS FOR TOPS QUILT

- ⁓ 1¾ yards of black print for second border
- ⁓ ⅝ yard of red solid for third border (2½ yards *total* combined with accent fabric)
- ⁓ ½ yard of green marbled print for first border
- ⁓ ⅔ yard of blue solid for binding
- ⁓ 3¾ yards of fabric for backing
- ⁓ 65" x 65" piece of batting

CUTTING

All measurements include ¼" seam allowances. Cut across the full width of the fabric unless otherwise specified.

From the green marbled print, cut:
5 strips, 2½" wide

From the red solid, cut:
8 strips, 2¼" wide

From the black print, cut on the *lengthwise* grain:
4 strips, 7" wide

From the blue solid, cut:
7 strips, 3" wide

ASSEMBLING THE QUILT TOP

1. Using the Tops triangles, make 36 blocks.

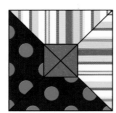

Make 36.

2. Arrange and sew the blocks together to make the quilt center as shown in the quilt diagram.

3. Cut one of the green strips in half. Sew each half strip to a full-length green strip.

4. Sew the red strips together in pairs.

5. Using the green strips for the first border, the black strips for the second border, and the red strips for the third border, sew each border to the quilt using the method for butted corners (page 91).

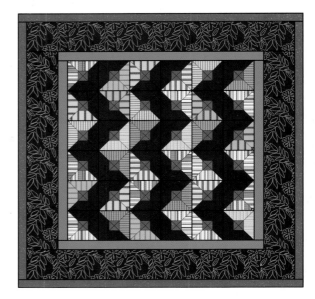

FINISHING THE QUILT

1. Cut and piece the backing fabric. Layer and baste the quilt top, batting, and backing.

2. Hand or machine quilt as desired.

3. Using the blue strips, prepare and sew the binding to the quilt.

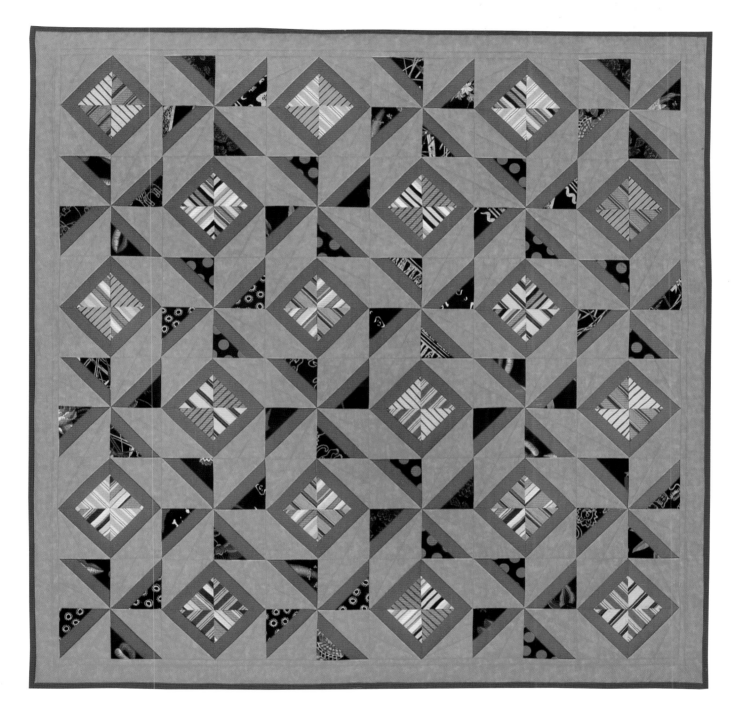

VAUDEVILLE: TAILS QUILT

Pieced and quilted by Judy Hooworth ~ Finished quilt: 61" x 61"

ADDITIONAL MATERIALS FOR TAILS QUILT

- 2½ yards of green marbled print for background and border
- ⅔ yard of blue solid for binding
- 3¾ yards of fabric for backing
- 65" x 65" piece of batting

CUTTING

All measurements include ¼" seam allowances. Cut across the full width of the fabric unless otherwise specified.

From the green print, cut:
11 strips, 5½" wide; crosscut into 72 squares, 5½" x 5½". Cut each square in half diagonally to make 144 half-square triangles.
7 strips, 2¾" wide

From the blue solid, cut:
7 strips, 3" wide

ASSEMBLING THE QUILT TOP

1. Using the Tails triangles and the green triangles, make 144 units, 72 using the black prints and 72 using the striped fabrics.

Make 72.   Make 72.

2. Make 18 blocks using the black units and 18 blocks using the striped units as shown. Use two different prints within each block.

 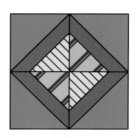

Make 18.   Make 18.

3. Arrange and sew the blocks together to make the quilt center as shown in the quilt photo on page 69.

4. Cut one of the 2¾"-wide green strips in half. Sew each half strip to a full-length 2¾"-wide green strip. Sew the four remaining green strips together in pairs.

5. Using the green strips, sew the border to the quilt using the method for butted corners (page 91).

FINISHING THE QUILT

1. Cut and piece the backing fabric. Layer and baste the quilt top, batting, and backing.

2. Hand or machine quilt as desired.

3. Using the blue strips, prepare and sew the binding to the quilt.

FABRIC TOTALS FOR BOTH QUILTS

If you plan to make both Vaudeville projects, the yardage below is enough to make both quilt tops and bindings.

- 12 fat eighths of bright striped fabrics*
- 12 fat eighths of black prints
- 2½ yards of red solid
- 2⅞ yards of green marbled print
- 1¾ yards of black print
- 1⅓ yards of blue solid

Stripes should go lengthwise down fabric; see "Using Stripes" (page 16).

Arbor Rose by Margaret Rolfe.
Tops: 63½" x 63½", *left.* ⌁ Tails: 65½" x 78½", *right.*

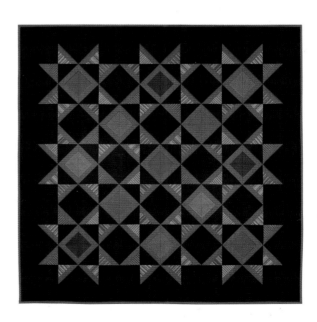

Indian Bazaar by Margaret Rolfe.
Tops: 58" x 62⅝", *left.* ⌁ Tails: 64½" x 64½", *right.*

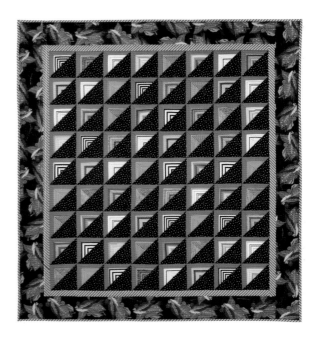

Neon Lights by Judy Hooworth.
Tops: 57½" x 57½", *left.* ⌁ Tails: 68" x 74½", *right.*

Springtime by Margaret Rolfe.
Tops: 58" x 58", *left.* ⌁ Tails: 50¼" x 59½", *right.*

Safari by Roslyn Dickens.
Tops: 50" x 50", *left.* ～ Tails: 58½" x 58½", *right.*

Waratah by Helene Saunders.
Tops: 51½" x 51½", *left.* ～ Tails: 55½" x 55½", *right.*

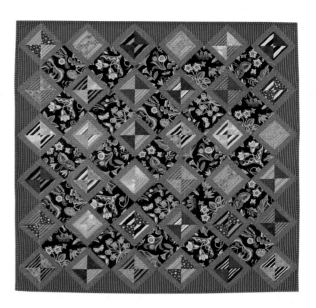

Licorice Allsorts by Wendy Knight. Quilted by Pru Singleton.
Tops: 55½" x 55½", *left.* ~ Tails: 54" x 54", *right.*

Pansy Passion by Heidi Nixon.
Tops: 55" x 55", quilted by Pru Singleton, *left.*
Tails: 68" x 68", quilted by Kaye Brown, *right.*

FANTASY GARDEN

Imagine a garden full of these glowing colors! The contrast between the two groups of fat quarters is created with florals in pinks and oranges and other prints in purples and blues. Thus the contrast is made with both color and value. The accent color is a bright blue.

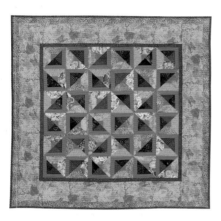

DOUBLES TRIANGLES

MATERIALS FOR THE DOUBLES TRIANGLES

- 6 fat quarters of florals in pinks and oranges

- 6 fat quarters of prints in purples and blues

- 1⅞ yards of blue solid for accent color

MAKING THE DOUBLES TRIANGLES

Following the instructions (pages 15–19), make the Tops and Tails triangles.

FANTASY GARDEN I

Pieced and quilted by Judy Hooworth ⮪ Finished quilt: 58" x 58"

ADDITIONAL MATERIALS FOR FANTASY GARDEN I

- 1⅔ yards of pink print for second border
- 1 yard of purple print for first border and binding
- ½ yard of orange print for third border
- 3⅝ yards of fabric for backing
- 62" x 62" piece of batting

CUTTING

All measurements include ¼" seam allowances. Cut across the full width of the fabric unless otherwise specified.

From the purple print, cut:
5 strips, 1½" wide
7 strips, 3" wide

From the orange print, cut:
6 strips, 2½" wide

From the pink print, cut on the *lengthwise* grain:
4 strips, 6½" wide

ASSEMBLING THE QUILT TOP

1. Using half of both the Tops and Tails triangles, make 36 blocks.

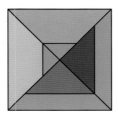

Make 36.

2. Arrange and sew the blocks together to make the quilt center as shown in the quilt diagram.

3. Cut one of the 1½"-wide purple strips into four equal pieces. Sew each quarter strip to a full-length 1½"-wide purple strip.

4. Cut two of the orange strips in half. Sew each half strip to a full-length orange strip.

5. Using the purple print for the first border, the pink print for the second border, and the orange print for the third border, attach the borders to the quilt using the method for butted corners (page 91). For this quilt, the side borders were added last.

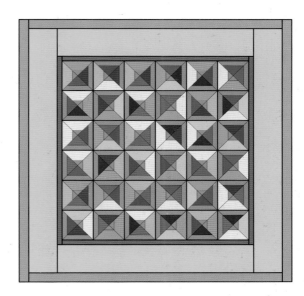

FINISHING THE QUILT

1. Cut and piece the backing fabric. Layer and baste the quilt top, batting, and backing.

2. Hand or machine quilt as desired.

3. Using the purple strips, prepare and sew the binding to the quilt.

FANTASY GARDEN II

Pieced and quilted by Judy Hooworth ～ Finished quilt: 48½" x 61½"

ADDITIONAL MATERIALS FOR FANTASY GARDEN II

- ~ 2 yards of blue print for second border
- ~ ⅜ yard of lilac print for first border
- ~ ⅝ yard of deep pink solid for binding
- ~ 3⅛ yards of fabric for backing
- ~ 53" x 66" piece of batting

CUTTING

All measurements include ¼" seam allowances. Cut across the full width of the fabric unless otherwise specified.

From the lilac print, cut:
5 strips, 2" wide

From the blue print, cut on the *lengthwise* grain:
4 strips, 6½" wide

From the deep pink solid, cut:
6 strips, 3" wide

ASSEMBLING THE QUILT TOP

1. Using half of the Tops and Tails triangles, make 35 blocks. (You'll have 4 extra triangles.)

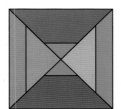

Make 35.

2. Arrange and sew the blocks together to make the quilt center as shown in the quilt diagram.

3. Cut one of the lilac strips in half. Sew each half strip to a full-length lilac strip.

4. Using the lilac strips for the first border and the blue strips for the second border, sew

the borders to the quilt using the method for mitered corners (page 91).

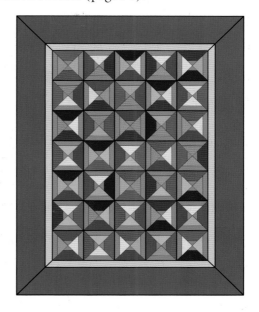

FINISHING THE QUILT

1. Cut and piece the backing fabric. Layer and baste the quilt top, batting, and backing.

2. Hand or machine quilt as desired.

3. Using the deep pink strips, prepare and sew the binding to the quilt.

FABRIC TOTALS FOR BOTH QUILTS

If you plan to make both Fantasy Garden projects, the yardage below is enough to make both quilt tops and bindings.

- ~ 6 fat quarters of pink and orange florals
- ~ 6 fat quarters of purple and blue prints
- ~ 1⅞ yards of blue solid
- ~ 2 yards of blue print
- ~ 1⅔ yards of pink print
- ~ 1 yard of purple print
- ~ ⅝ yard of deep pink solid
- ~ ½ yard of orange print
- ~ ⅜ yard of lilac print

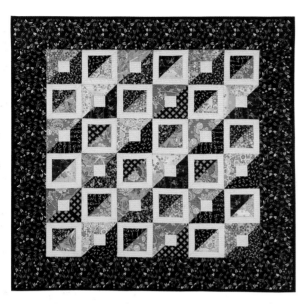

Indigo Autumn by Margaret Rolfe.
Quilt I: 52" x 52", *left.* ～ Quilt II: 52" x 52", *right.*

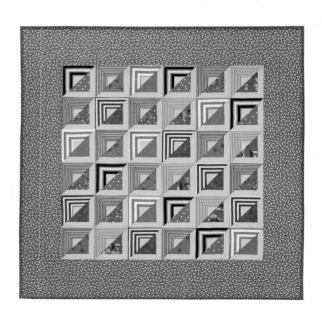

Primary Colors by Judy Hooworth and Margaret Rolfe.
Quilt I: 52" x 52", *left.* ～ Quilt II: 55" x 55", *right.*

FALLING WATER

The Sides triangles used in this quilt came from "Falling Water" (page 45).

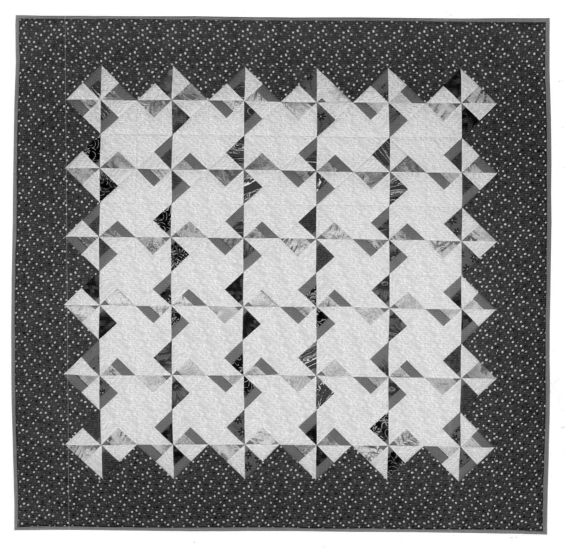

Pieced and quilted by Judy Hooworth
Finished quilt: 64" x 64"

MATERIALS

~ 144 Sides triangles from "Falling Water" (72 Sides-Tops and 72 Sides-Tails triangles; see page 45)

~ 2 yards of blue print for setting triangles and border

~ 1⅞ yards of yellow print for Pinwheel and alternate blocks

~ ⅔ yard of red solid for binding

~ 4 yards of fabric for backing

~ 68" x 68" piece of batting

CUTTING

All measurements include ¼" seam allowances. Cut across the full width of the fabric unless otherwise specified.

From the yellow print, cut:
5 strips, 6½" wide; crosscut into 25 squares, 6½" x 6½". Trim the remainder of the last strip to 3⅞" wide.
7 strips, 3⅞" wide; crosscut these and the remainder of the above strip into 72 squares, 3⅞" x 3⅞". Cut each square in half diagonally to make a total of 144 half-square triangles.

From the blue print, cut on the *lengthwise* grain:
4 strips, 6½" wide
1 strip, 9¾" wide; crosscut into 5 squares, 9¾" x 9¾". Cut each square diagonally twice to make 20 quarter-square triangles. Trim the remainder of the strip to 5⅛" wide and crosscut into 2 squares, 5⅛" x 5⅛". Cut each square in half diagonally to make 4 half-square triangles.

From the red solid, cut:
7 strips, 3" wide

ASSEMBLING THE QUILT TOP

1. Using the Sides triangles and the 3⅞" yellow triangles, make 144 units as shown.

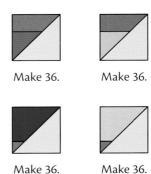

Make 36.   Make 36.

Make 36.   Make 36.

2. Make 36 blocks, 18 using the Tops units and 18 using the Tails units from step 1.

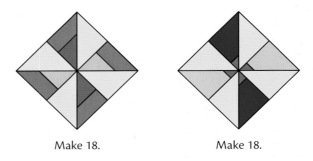

Make 18.   Make 18.

3. Arrange the pieced blocks, the yellow squares, and the blue side and corner setting triangles to make the quilt center as shown in the quilt photo on page 81. Sew all these together, using a diagonal construction.

4. Using the blue strips, attach the border to the quilt using the method for butted corners (page 91).

FINISHING THE QUILT

1. Cut and piece the backing fabric. Layer and baste the quilt top, batting, and backing.

2. Hand or machine quilt as desired.

3. Using the red strips, prepare and sew the binding to the quilt.

FANTASY GARDEN
SIDES-TOPS QUILT

Use the Sides-Tops triangles from the Fantasy Garden quilts (page 75) to make blocks reminiscent of the Birds in the Air block. See the next quilt for how to use the Sides-Tails triangles.

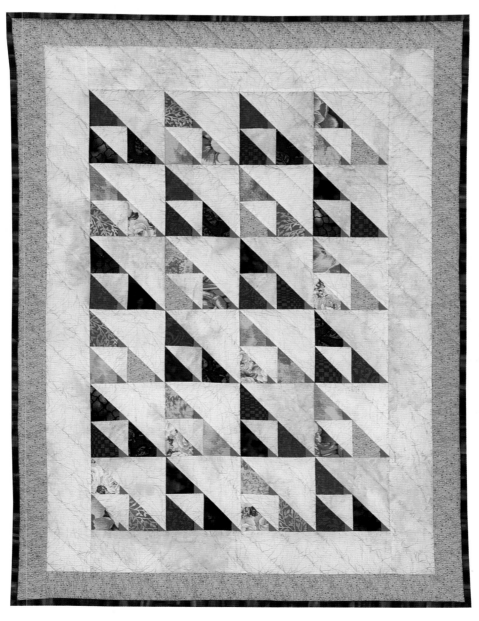

Pieced and quilted by Judy Hooworth
Finished quilt: 36½" x 48½"

Note: For more efficient use of fabric, the instructions are written so that the side border strips are added first.

MATERIALS

~ 72 Sides-Tops triangles from "Fantasy Garden" (page 75)

~ 1⅓ yards of yellow print for background and first border

~ ½ yard of pink print for second border

~ ½ yard of blue print for binding

~ 2½ yards* of fabric for backing

~ 41" x 53" piece of batting

If your fabric is at least 41" wide after prewashing, 1⅔ yards will be enough.

CUTTING

All measurements include ¼" seam allowances. Cut across the full width of the fabric unless otherwise specified.

From the yellow print, cut:
4 strips, 4" wide
3 strips, 6⅞" wide; crosscut into 12 squares, 6⅞" x 6⅞". Cut each square in half diagonally to make a total of 24 half-square triangles. Trim the remainder of the third strip to 3⅞" wide.
1 strip, 3⅞" wide; crosscut this and the remainder of the strip above into 12 squares, 3⅞" x 3⅞". Cut each square in half diagonally to make a total of 24 half-square triangles.

From the pink print, cut:
5 strips, 2¾" wide

From the blue print, cut:
5 strips, 3" wide

ASSEMBLING THE QUILT TOP

1. Using the Sides-Tops triangles and the 3⅞" yellow print and 6⅞" yellow print triangles, make 24 blocks, 12 blocks using the pink and orange prints and 12 blocks using the blue and purple prints.

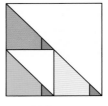 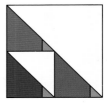

Make 12.   Make 12.

2. Arrange and sew the quilt blocks together to make the quilt center as shown in the quilt diagram.

3. Cut one of the pink strips in half. Sew each half strip to a full-length pink strip.

4. Using the yellow strips for the first border and the pink strips for the second border, attach the borders to the quilt using the method for butted corners (page 91).

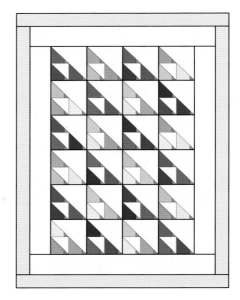

FINISHING THE QUILT

1. Cut and piece the backing fabric. Layer and baste the quilt top, batting, and backing.

2. Hand or machine quilt as desired.

3. Using the blue strips, prepare and sew the binding to the quilt.

FANTASY GARDEN
SIDES-TAILS QUILT

Here's a quilt that uses the Sides-Tails triangles from the Fantasy Garden quilts (page 75).

Pieced and quilted by Judy Hooworth
Finished quilt: 43" x 55"

MATERIALS

- 72 Sides-Tails triangles from "Fantasy Garden" (page 75)
- 1⅓ yards of white tone-on-tone print for Pinwheel blocks and pieced border
- 1⅓ yards of blue print for alternate blocks and pieced border
- ⅝ yard of blue solid for binding
- 2¾ yards of fabric for backing
- 47" x 59" piece of batting

CUTTING

All measurements include ¼" seam allowances. Cut across the full width of the fabric unless otherwise specified.

From the white tone-on-tone print, cut on the *lengthwise* **grain:**
8 strips, 2½" wide
4 strips, 3⅞" wide; crosscut into 36 squares, 3⅞" x 3⅞". Cut each square in half diagonally to make a total of 72 half-square triangles.

From the blue print, cut on the *lengthwise* **grain:**
4 strips, 2½" wide
3 strips, 6½" wide; crosscut into 17 squares, 6½" x 6½"

From the blue solid, cut:
6 strips, 3" wide

ASSEMBLING THE QUILT TOP

1. Using the Sides-Tails triangles and the 3⅞" white triangles, make 72 units, 36 using the blue and purple prints and 36 using the pink and orange prints.

Make 36.   Make 36.

2. Make 18 Pinwheel blocks using the units from step 1.

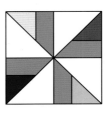

Make 18.

3. Arrange and sew the quilt blocks together to make the quilt center as shown in the quilt diagram.

4. Sew the white tone-on-tone and blue print strips together into groups of three, with white on the outside.

5. Using the pieced strips, attach the border to the quilt, using the method for butted corners (page 91).

FINISHING THE QUILT

1. Cut and piece the backing fabric. Layer and baste the quilt top, batting, and backing.

2. Hand or machine quilt as desired.

3. Using the blue solid strips, prepare and sew the binding to the quilt.

Bunting by Judy Hooworth, 53" x 53"

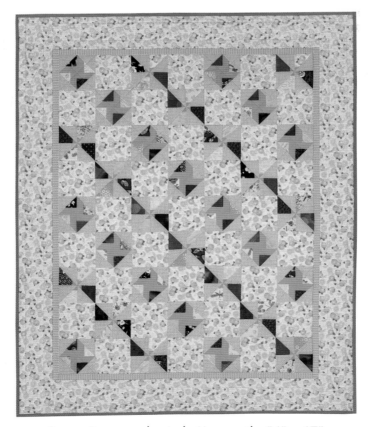

Sunny Provence by Judy Hooworth, 56" x 67"

Refer to this section for specific information on materials, supplies, and quiltmaking techniques.

FABRIC

Use cotton fabric for the quilt tops and backs, prewashing all fabric to avoid any shrinkage or color running later. All fabric quantities in materials lists are based on approximately 42"-wide fabric, with 40" being usable after washing and removing selvages.

EQUIPMENT

The usual sewing equipment is required, including fabric scissors, pins, hand-sewing needles, and a seam ripper.

Sewing machine. A sewing machine is needed for piecing, quilt assembly, and machine quilting. Set your machine for a straight stitch and use a ¼" presser foot to maintain accurate ¼" seam allowances. For machine quilting, use a walking foot or dual feed mechanism. For free-motion quilting, use a darning or free-motion quilting foot.

Rotary-cutting tools. You need a rotary cutter and a mat that is at least 17" x 23". For cutting strips, use a 6" x 24" ruler. For cutting the Doubles triangles, use a 6" or 6½" square ruler OR a special ruler for cutting quarter-square triangles.

Iron. Use a dry iron when pressing the blocks so that you can change the direction of the seam allowances if needed. For other pressing, steam may be used.

Design wall. Use a design wall to try out different arrangements of triangles or to audition different fabrics for borders and bindings. A large pin board covered with felt or flannel is ideal. Or, simply hang up a large sheet of flannel.

Quilting supplies. For machine quilting, several hundred safety pins are required for pin basting the quilt layers. For hand quilting, use a darning needle for basting and a Between needle for quilting. Protect your fingers with thimbles or finger protectors, and use a quilting frame or hoop to support the quilt. To mark quilting designs, use a chalk marker, a pencil suitable for marking fabric, or a No. 2 pencil. You can also use masking tape to mark straight lines when hand quilting.

ROTARY CUTTING

To ensure accuracy, iron all fabric before cutting. If the fabric is larger than the mat, fold the fabric before cutting. If you are cutting across the width of the fabric, fold the fabric in half, selvage edge to selvage edge. If cutting down the length of the fabric, make as many folds along the length as required for the fabric to fit on the cutting mat.

The cutting sizes for all pieces include ¼" seam allowances. The term *finished size* refers to the size of a piece of patchwork without seam allowances, that is, the size it will appear in the finished quilt.

All cutting is done across the width of the fabric unless there is a specific instruction to cut lengthwise down the fabric.

The following diagrams show right-handed cutting. Follow the instructions in reverse if you are left-handed.

Cutting strips. Begin by cutting one edge of the fabric straight. If the fabric is folded, make sure that the cut is at a 90° angle to the fold.

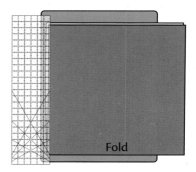

Fold

Measuring carefully from the cut edge, cut strips the required width. Because it is necessary to cut from the straightened edge, either rotate the cutting mat 180° or move around to the other side. Note that from time to time it will be necessary to check that your cutting is still 90° to the fold. Recut to straighten the edge as required.

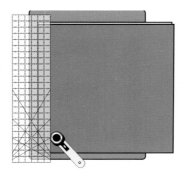

Cutting squares and rectangles. Make squares and rectangles by crosscutting the strips. First, square up one end of the strip by making a cut that is exactly 90° to the long edge of the strip. Measuring from this straight edge, cut the sizes required.

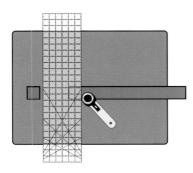

Cutting half-square triangles. Make half-square triangles by cutting squares in half diagonally.

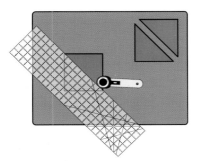

Cutting quarter-square triangles. Make quarter-square triangles by cutting squares twice diagonally. Be careful not to disturb the pieces from the first cut when making the second diagonal cut.

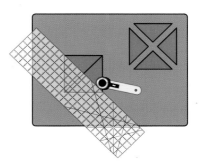

MEASUREMENTS FOR ROTARY CUTTING

All our cutting measurements include the ¼" seam allowances, but sometimes you may need to figure your own measurements.

To cut squares and rectangles, cut each shape ½" larger than the finished size.

Squares and rectangles: add ½"

To cut half-square triangles, cut a square ⅞" larger than the finished size of a square made of two half-square triangles.

Half-square triangles: add ⅞"

To cut quarter-square triangles, cut a square 1¼" larger than the finished size of a square made of four quarter-square triangles.

Quarter-square triangles: add 1¼"

PIECING AND PRESSING

An accurate ¼" seam allowance is essential for all piecing. The pieces will not fit together properly unless a ¼" seam allowance is both cut and sewn.

Seam allowances are pressed to one side while piecing. When seam allowances are pressed in opposite directions at seam intersections, the join will be more accurate and flat. Plan your pressing with this principle in mind.

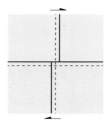

To make fabric joins as invisible as possible, for example, when joining strips to make borders or bindings, press the seam allowances open.

QUILT ASSEMBLY

After arranging your blocks on a design wall, you're ready to assemble your quilt.

1. Sew the blocks into rows, pressing the seam allowances of the rows in alternate directions. Label the rows with numbers to avoid mix-ups.

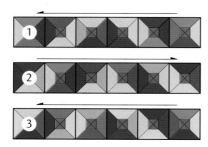

2. Sew the rows together, pinning at the seam junctions for accuracy.

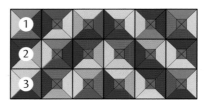

Diagonal Construction

When the blocks are set on point, sew the quilt in diagonal rows. Setting triangles are used at the sides and corners to make the quilt square.

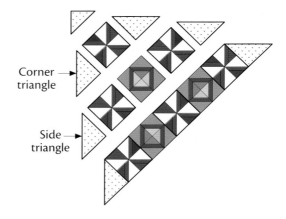

Blocks with Sashing

For sashing with sashing cornerstones, sew the bocks in rows with the sashing strips between the blocks, pressing seam allowances toward the sashing strips. Sew the sashing strips and cornerstones into rows, again pressing the seam allowances towards the sashing strips. Pin and stitch the rows together, alternating the rows of sashing and cornerstones with the rows of blocks.

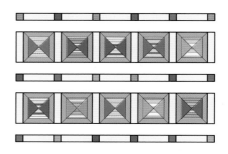

ADDING BORDERS

Choose fabrics for borders by "auditioning" them—that is, by trying out different fabrics to see what works best. Pin the center of the quilt top to your design wall and then pin lengths of fabric next to it, folding or overlapping the fabrics to show approximate widths. Some quilts need only one border, but others need two or more to enhance the center piecing. Think carefully about the width of each border. Sometimes only a narrow strip of a color is all that is necessary to add zing.

Choose either butted or mitered corners on the basis of what best suits the quilt top and the fabrics. Striped fabrics may look better with mitered corners. If the quilt blocks are set on point, the diagonal directions of the seams may suggest a mitered corner. If the border fabric is directional, butted corners may be in order.

Always measure the borders carefully, matching the center measurements of the quilt top to make quilts that are both flat and square at the corners.

Butted Corners

1. Square up one end of the strips for the side borders; then lay the strips down the center length of the quilt, matching the squared-up ends to the top edge of the quilt. Pin-mark the border strips at the bottom edge of the quilt. Trim the border strips to this length. Pin-mark the center of the borders and the center sides of the quilt.

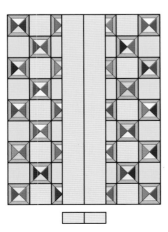

2. Pin the borders to each side of the quilt, first pinning at the ends and then pinning the middle, matching the center pin marks. Continue to add pins along the border until it is evenly pinned. Stitch the borders to the quilt and press the seam allowances toward the borders.

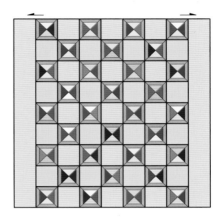

3. Measure and trim the top and bottom borders by laying them across the center width of the quilt top, including the newly added side borders.

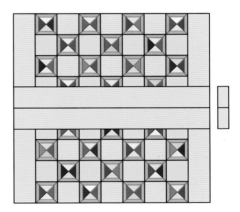

4. Pin and stitch the top and bottom borders to the quilt. Press the seam allowances toward the borders.

5. If there are multiple borders, repeat the steps for each border.

Mitered Corners

Cut border strips for mitered borders by measuring the finished length of the border and adding 4".

1. Pin-mark the centers of each side of the quilt and the centers of each border strip. Lay the top and botom border strips across the center of the quilt, matching the centers. Pin-mark the borders at the edge of the quilt.

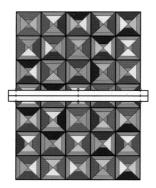

2. Pin the borders to the quilt, matching the center pins and matching the edges of the quilt top to the pins on the border strips. Sew the strips to the quilt, being careful to start and stop sewing exactly ¼" inside the edges of the quilt.

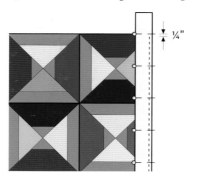

3. Repeat steps 1 and 2 for the side borders.

4. Working on each corner in turn, use a pencil and ruler to mark a 45° angle from the end of the stitching to the edge of the border on both ends of each border strip. Matching the pencil lines, pin the borders together and stitch.

5. Trim away excess fabric and press the seam open.

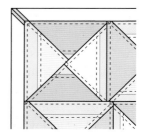

MITERING MULTIPLE BORDERS

For multiple borders, sew the border strips together first and treat them as a unit. Pin-mark all border strips in the center, match the centers, and sew the strips together.

Then follow the steps for a single mitered border, and carefully match the seams of the border strips at the miter.

Striped Borders

Always pin-mark the center of a striped border *in the center of a stripe* so that the stripes will fall at the same place at both ends.

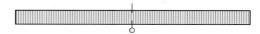

LAYERING AND BASTING

Make backings the size of the quilt top plus 4". Remove the selvage edges. Measure and cut the fabric into the number of lengths needed; then sew the lengths together. Press the seam allowances open. Trim the backing to the required size.

Press the backing and quilt top so that they are wrinkle free. If you want to mark quilting lines with a pencil, do it at this time. (With a chalk marker, wait until just before stitching.)

Lay the backing out in a clear space, right side down. If the work surface is slippery, use masking tape to hold the backing in place. Lay the batting over the backing, and then lay the quilt top over the batting, right side up. Make sure there are no wrinkles in any layer. For all our quilts we chose a mid-loft polyester batting that did not require close quilting.

Quilting by machine. Using safety pins, place pins over the surface of the quilt, 3" to 4" apart. Plan the placement so that the pins are not in the way of the quilting lines. Pin in two stages. First, put in all the safety pins without closing them. Then go back and close all the pins. This prevents shifting of the quilt layers as you close the pins.

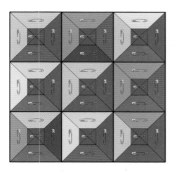

Quilting by hand. Using thread and a darning needle, baste a grid of long running stitches over the surface of the quilt. Begin in the center and stitch out to the four sides; then fill in the whole quilt with a 3" to 4" grid.

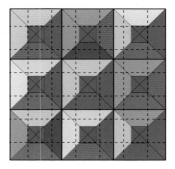

QUILTING

Quilting by hand or machine is a personal preference—do what you enjoy best! These quilts lend themselves to simple quilting.

BINDING

Margaret and Judy have different binding methods. Judy makes a continuous binding, and Margaret prefers to bind each side separately.

Prepare the quilt for binding by pinning and stay stitching around the edge of the quilt, stitching ⅛" inside the raw edges of the quilt top. Trim the batting and backing so they are ¼" wider than the quilt top all around. Make sure that the corners are trimmed square. The binding strips for the quilts in this book are all cut 3" wide, making a finished binding width of ½".

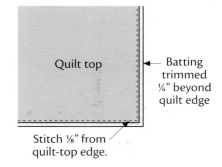

Continuous Binding

1. Join the binding strips into one length using a diagonal or crosswise seam. (Always use a crosswise seam for striped fabrics.) Press the seam allowances open. Then fold the strip in half lengthwise with wrong sides together and press to make a double-fold binding.

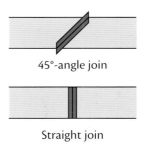

45°-angle join

Straight join

2. Begin stitching at the center bottom of the quilt, leaving 6" of the binding free to make the join at the end. Align the raw edges of the binding with the raw edge of the quilt top, and stitch with a ¼" seam allowance (note that the batting and backing will extend ¼" beyond the edge of the quilt top). Be careful not to stretch the quilt as you sew.

3. Stitch the binding strip, stopping exactly ¼" from the edge of the quilt top (½" from the edge of the trimmed batting and backing), and end by taking a few stitches in reverse. Cut the threads.

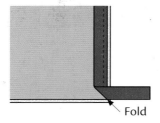

Stitch to ¼" from quilt-top edge (½" from edge of batting).

4. Fold the binding away from the center of the quilt so that the fold forms a 45° angle. The cut edges of the binding will be in line with the next side of the quilt top.

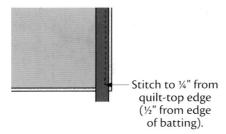

Fold

5. Fold the binding back on itself, aligning the fold with the trimmed edge of the batting and backing. The cut edges of the binding should again be in line with the next side of the quilt top. Begin stitching at the edge of the fold and stitch the next side of the quilt.

Fold

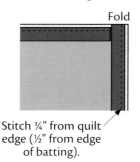

Stitch ¼" from quilt edge (½" from edge of batting).

6. Continue stitching around the quilt, sewing each corner in the same way. Stop stitching 6" before you meet the stitching at the beginning.

7. Join the ends of the binding, making either a diagonal or crosswise seam as follows.

To make a diagonal seam: Trim the ends of the binding so that they overlap by exactly 3" (the width of the binding strip).

Trim overlap to 3".

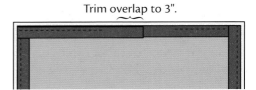

Open out the fold in the binding and sew the strips together with a diagonal seam. Trim and press the seam allowances open.

Stitch ends together on a 45° angle.

To make a crosswise seam: Fold and finger-press the binding back on itself to mark the joining point. Trim a seam allowance on each end to ¼" beyond the finger-pressed fold.

Finger-press folds and trim ¼" seam allowances.

Open out the fold in the binding and sew the strips together with a crosswise seam. Press the seam allowances open.

Stitch the binding to the quilt across the join. Fold the binding over to the back and hand stitch into place, folding the corners neatly.

Binding Separate Sides

1. Follow step 1 of "Continuous Binding" (page 93), joining binding strips as required for the lengths of each border.

2. Add the side bindings first, measuring through the center of the quilt to determine the length needed. Pin-mark the binding strips to this length. Pin the binding to the quilt, matching the marked ends of the binding to the edges of the quilt. Pin evenly along the length of the binding, placing pins about 2" apart. Sew the binding in place, remove pins, and trim the ends even with the quilt. Fold the binding to the back of the quilt and pin in place.

3. Repeat the same process for the top and bottom of the quilt, measuring the width of the quilt through the center. After sewing, trim the binding strips so that they extend ½" beyond each side of the quilt.

4. Fold the binding to the back of the quilt, folding the corners neatly. Pin and hand stitch the binding in place.

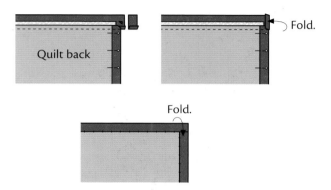

RESOURCES

For a comprehensive guide to patchwork and quiltmaking, see *The Magic of Quiltmaking: A Beginner's Guide* by Margaret Rolfe and Jenny Bowker (Martingale & Company, 2004).

METRIC EQUIVALENTS

The measurements used in *Quilts on the Double* cannot be converted cleanly into metric measurements, so imperial measurements must be used. For those who buy fabrics in metric quantities, the equivalents in the chart at right may be useful. Note that these are not exact equivalents, because they have been rounded up to a practical size.

IMPERIAL	METRIC
1"	2.5 cm
2"	5 cm
4"	10 cm
4½" (⅛ yard)	12 cm
9" (¼ yard)	25 cm
12" (⅓ yard)	35 cm
13½" (⅜ yard)	35 cm
18" (½ yard)	50 cm
22½" (⅝ yard)	60 cm
27" (¾ yard)	70 cm
31½" (⅞ yard)	80 cm
36" (1 yard)	95 cm
40"	105 cm
1½ yards	1.4 m
2 yards	1.9 m
3 yards	2.8 m
4 yards	3.8 m

Judy Hooworth is a leading Australian quiltmaker. She started out as an art teacher but became fascinated with the American quilts that she saw in magazines in the 1960s and 1970s. Judy began to make quilts herself, learning as she went. While she has always loved traditional quilts, Judy also began to make her own contemporary quilts. From these beginnings, Judy has continued with this double focus— making pieced quilts with a modern twist and making art quilts of her own unique design.

Judy is renowned for her bold and brilliant use of color. Her quilts have been exhibited in Australia and around the world, including Quilt National four times. Judy has taught patchwork and quilting in Australia and around the world, and she has written two previous books, *Razzle Dazzle Quilts* (Martingale & Company, 2001) and *Spectacular Scraps: A Simple Approach to Stunning Quilts* (Martingale & Company, 1999), coauthored with Margaret Rolfe. Judy lives in Morisset, which is north of Sydney, with her husband, Richard, and two cats.

Margaret Rolfe is also a leading Australian quiltmaker. She was inspired to make quilts after being introduced to patchwork while visiting America in 1975. Returning to Australia, she also had to learn by doing. Margaret began teaching and writing books in the 1980s, and she has become well known for her pieced designs of animals and birds. Many of these designs are in her bestselling book *A Quilter's Ark* (Martingale & Company, 1997). She has always been interested in the history of quilting in Australia and has written several books on this subject. Her most recent books are *Successful Scrap Quilts from Simple Rectangles* (Martingale & Company, 2002), coauthored with Judy Turner, and *The Magic of Quiltmaking: A Beginner's Guide* (Martingale & Company, 2004), coauthored with Jenny Bowker. In 2001 Margaret was nationally honored by becoming a Member of the Order of Australia. Margaret lives in Canberra, Australia's capital, with her husband, Barry, and two dogs.

Judy and Margaret became friends while working on their previous book *Spectacular Scraps*. They are especially delighted to be collaborating again with this book, because it continues their shared love of pieced quilts and the exploration of pattern.